T0329403

CAMBRIDGE LIBRARY COLLECTION

Books of enduring scholarly value

Polar Exploration

This series includes accounts, by eye-witnesses and contemporaries, of early expeditions to the Arctic and the Antarctic. Huge resources were invested in such endeavours, particularly the search for the North-West Passage, which, if successful, promised enormous strategic and commercial rewards. Cartographers and scientists travelled with many of the expeditions, and their work made important contributions to earth sciences, climatology, botany and zoology. They also brought back anthropological information about the indigenous peoples of the Arctic region and the southern fringes of the American continent. The series further includes dramatic and poignant accounts of the harsh realities of working in extreme conditions and utter isolation in bygone centuries.

The Royal Geographical Society and the Arctic Expedition of 1875–6

The enthusiasm of Sir Clements R. Markham (1830–1916) for travel and exploration started early and took him around the world. Originally a naval officer, he was later responsible for organising the geographical mapping of much of India, and brought the method of brewing pure quinine to India from his extensive travels in Peru. An active and influential member of the Hakluyt Society and Royal Geographical Society, Markham was instrumental in gathering support for this 1875–6 Arctic expedition. He gives a clear account of the funding, planning and aims, the execution of the journey, and how the research should be continued. In particular, he documents the physical activities involved on the expedition, including the surveying of coastal landforms, and the tradition of the Royal Navy in the Arctic. This 1877 template for scientific exploration demonstrates the approaches adopted in the nineteenth century, and is still of interest today.

Cambridge University Press has long been a pioneer in the reissuing of out-of-print titles from its own backlist, producing digital reprints of books that are still sought after by scholars and students but could not be reprinted economically using traditional technology. The Cambridge Library Collection extends this activity to a wider range of books which are still of importance to researchers and professionals, either for the source material they contain, or as landmarks in the history of their academic discipline.

Drawing from the world-renowned collections in the Cambridge University Library and other partner libraries, and guided by the advice of experts in each subject area, Cambridge University Press is using state-of-the-art scanning machines in its own Printing House to capture the content of each book selected for inclusion. The files are processed to give a consistently clear, crisp image, and the books finished to the high quality standard for which the Press is recognised around the world. The latest print-on-demand technology ensures that the books will remain available indefinitely, and that orders for single or multiple copies can quickly be supplied.

The Cambridge Library Collection brings back to life books of enduring scholarly value (including out-of-copyright works originally issued by other publishers) across a wide range of disciplines in the humanities and social sciences and in science and technology.

The Royal Geographical Society and the Arctic Expedition of 1875–6

A Report

CLEMENTS ROBERT MARKHAM

CAMBRIDGE UNIVERSITY PRESS

Cambridge, New York, Melbourne, Madrid, Cape Town,
Singapore, São Paolo, Delhi, Mexico City

Published in the United States of America by Cambridge University Press, New York

www.cambridge.org
Information on this title: www.cambridge.org/9781108049719

© in this compilation Cambridge University Press 2012

This edition first published 1877
This digitally printed version 2012

ISBN 978-1-108-04971-9 Paperback

THE

ROYAL GEOGRAPHICAL SOCIETY

AND

THE ARCTIC EXPEDITION OF 1875–76.

A REPORT.

BY

CLEMENTS R. MARKHAM, C.B., F.R.S.,

SECRETARY OF THE ROYAL GEOGRAPHICAL SOCIETY.

LONDON:

PRINTED BY WILLIAM CLOWES AND SONS,

STAMFORD STREET AND CHARING CROSS.

1877.

TABLE OF CONTENTS.

———•‹•———

I.

HISTORY OF THE EFFORTS TO OBTAIN A RENEWAL OF ARCTIC RESEARCH.

II.

SUCCESSFUL RESULTS OF THE ARCTIC EXPEDITION OF 1875–76.

III.

ROUTES FOR FUTURE ARCTIC EXPEDITIONS.

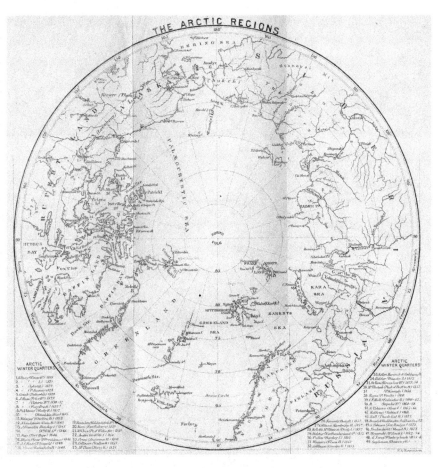

The material originally positioned here is too large for reproduction in this reissue. A PDF can be downloaded from the web address given on page iv of this book, by clicking on 'Resources Available'.

THE ROYAL GEOGRAPHICAL SOCIETY

AND

THE ARCTIC EXPEDITION OF 1875-76.

I.

HISTORY OF THE EFFORTS TO OBTAIN A RENEWAL OF ARCTIC RESEARCH.

WHEN, in 1865, the Council of the Royal Geographical Society undertook to advocate and promote the exploration of the unknown region round the Pole, it was fully understood that the great work could only be accomplished gradually, and that one expedition must follow another until all the knowledge attainable by human means, in this field of inquiry, had been obtained. One important step in advance has been made by the discoveries of the Arctic Expedition of 1875-6; and it now becomes necessary to take stock of our increased knowledge, and by its light to consider the next step in advance that should be advocated.

2. The duty of thus summing up the case, at the termination of the first effort, would have fallen upon our lamented Associate, Admiral Sherard Osborn, had he been spared to us. He it was who first raised the question in 1865, who perseveringly and ably kept it alive, who by his winning eloquence and well-deserved influence won adherents, and who at length secured the despatch of an expedition by the route which he had advocated for ten years. His efforts were crowned with complete success, in the very year that he died. The cause of Arctic discovery has sustained a loss which cannot be replaced. We can no longer be sustained by that help which never failed; yet the memory of Osborn's cheery voice, and hearty joyous smile, which won upon men's feelings nearly as much as his close reasoning and well-marshalled facts affected their judgments, will nerve us still to do battle in the same noble cause.

3. I have undertaken the duty thus left undone, partly as Secretary of the Geographical Society, which has made this cause its own, and partly as the constant assistant and adviser of Sherard Osborn

from the day when he began to advocate the renewal of Arctic research in 1865, until the day of his death. We had been mess-mates during four years, we had served together in the same Arctic Expedition, and our friendship had stood the test of thirty years. When Osborn went to Bombay in March 1865, he entrusted all his notes and correspondence on the Arctic question to me, and he did so again on a later occasion. Together we discussed each point as it arose, every step that should be taken, and together we prepared the memoranda, drafts of letters, and reports which were adopted by the Council of the Geographical Society. So that the duty of discussing the question at the point it has now reached, which would have belonged to Osborn if he had been spared to us, does not unnaturally fall upon one who, in this matter, was his coadjutor and assistant.

4. It will be well, before marshalling our new knowledge, to recapitulate the history of our efforts to obtain a renewal of Arctic exploration, since their commencement in 1865.

5. In determining the policy to be pursued for securing the despatch of an Arctic Expedition, it was above all things neces-sary to ascertain the points which former Arctic experience had firmly established, and to formulate them, so as to have a firm stand-point from whence to start.

6. This experience bears upon the two main divisions of the sub-ject, namely, the objects of Arctic exploration, and the means of securing those objects.

7. Formerly, and since 1775, the objects, or at least the main ob-jects, of Arctic voyages had been to make the North-west Passage or to reach the North Pole. The last voyage for the former object left England in 1845, and for the latter in 1827. But the advance of knowledge had since proved that there could be no useful and tangible results either in making the North-west Passage or in reaching the North Pole. These objects had, therefore, to be finally discarded. It was quite clear that Arctic discovery would have no influential support from any of the learned Societies, without which success was impossible, if to reach the North Pole—an utterly useless quest—was its main object.

8. The objects of Arctic exploration, in these days, must be to secure useful scientific results; in geography by exploring the coast lines and ascertaining the conditions of land and sea within the unknown area; in geology by collections and by a careful examination of the land; in zoology and botany by observation and by collections; in physics by a complete series of observations extending over at least a year.

9. Such being the scientific objects of Arctic exploration, they must be kept in mind when the rules for securing them, based upon long experience, are formulated. But there is another object which had great weight with Sherard Osborn. He specially dwelt upon the importance of encouraging a spirit of maritime enterprise, and of giving worthy employment to the navy in time of peace—a truly national object, and one which, as the result proved, had as much influence in forming the decision of statesmen as the scientific results.

10. We now come to the means whereby the unknown Polar area is to be penetrated, and the desired success to be secured. The first great lesson taught by two centuries of experience is that no extensive and useful exploring work can be calculated upon by merely entering the drifting pack; and that effective progress can be made only by following a coast line. The second Arctic canon is that, to secure efficient work, at least one winter must be faced in a position beyond any point hitherto reached. This is essential in order to obtain series of observations of any value. The third rule is that mere navigation in a ship cannot secure the results desired from Arctic exploration, and that it must be supplemented by sledge travelling. The exploration of 50 miles of coast by a sledge party is worth more to science than the discovery of 500 miles of sea or coast by a ship. In the former case the land is accurately mapped, and its fauna, flora, geology, and physical features are ascertained. In the latter a coast is seen and its outline shown by a dotted line on a chart, and that is all. The two methods will not bear comparison.

11. The experience of centuries of Arctic research has thus resulted in the establishment of three canons, which form unerring guides to us who inherit that experience:

1. Navigate along a coast line, and avoid the drifting pack.

2. It is necessary to pass at least one winter at a point beyond any hitherto reached.

3. The ships must be looked upon merely as the base of operations, and sledges as the main instruments for discovery and exploration.

12. With the objects of Arctic research, and the means of securing those objects thus distinctly formulated; the next point was to decide by which route leading to the unknown area round the North Pole, those essential conditions could best be found. In the first place, there must be coast lines leading into the unknown space both for navigation and for sledge travelling. In the second place, there must be a prospect of finding suitable winter quarters beyond the threshold of the hitherto discovered region. At that

time, Smith Sound, and the east coast of Greenland, alone met such
conditions. Of these two, Smith Sound offered two coast lines for
exploration instead of one; its navigation was believed to be less
difficult, and to offer a better chance of securing winter quarters
beyond the threshold of the unknown region, and finally the
means of retreat, in case of disaster, were better by that route.
The Smith Sound route was consequently the best by which to
commence the discovery of the vast unknown area.

13. This was the train of reasoning by which we arrived at the
conclusion, that to secure the true objects of Arctic discovery, and
to make a successful commencement of the examination of the unknown area, the first expedition should proceed by the route of
Smith Sound.

14. On the 23rd of January, 1865, after all these points had been
most carefully investigated and considered, Sherard Osborn read
his first paper at a memorable meeting of the Geographical Society,
on the exploration of the North Polar Region.˙ His proposal was
that two steamers should be despatched to Smith Sound, that one
should winter near Cape Isabella, and that the other should press
up the western shore as far as possible. In the following spring,
sledge operations were to be directed over the unknown area.
Osborn also enumerated the valuable results to be secured from
Arctic exploration.

15. In the long and interesting discussion which followed the
reading of the paper, the views of Sherard Osborn received cordial support from Sir Roderick Murchison, General Sabine, Captain
R. V. Hamilton, Captain Inglefield, and Dr. Donnet. They were
opposed by Captain Richards, the hydrographer.

16. But in March 1865, Osborn was obliged to go to Bombay,
leaving the cause in my less experienced hands, and an opposition
commenced, the text of which was two letters from Dr. Petermann.
On April 10th, 1865, I read a paper at a meeting of the Geographical Society on the best route for North Polar exploration, in
which I added some fresh arguments in support of Osborn's views.
But Dr. Petermann's letters were also read, and, almost single-
handed (supported only by Sir George Back and Admiral Collinson), I had to defend the position against a number of Dr. Petermann's English supporters. These letters, which proved to be a
disastrous apple of discord, might now be advantageously for-
gotten, if they had not been quite recently upheld, by Admiral
Richards, as models of wisdom and logical reasoning.* This makes

* In the discussion after the reading of Sir George Nares's Paper, on March 26,
1877.

it desirable that a refutation of each point in the two letters should be submitted.

17. Dr. Petermann's letters were written to advocate the Spitzbergen route for Polar exploration, that is, the despatch of vessels to the open pack, away from the land, to the north of the Spitzbergen group. In his first letter he assigns eight reasons for his preference for this route. The first is that the voyage from England to the North Pole is shorter by Spitzbergen; a matter which might be important to a company wishing to establish a line of packets between the two points, but which has no bearing on the question of exploration. The second is that the Spitzbergen sea forms the widest entrance to the unknown region. This is one of the strongest objections to the route, for the navigation must be conducted in a drifting pack away from land. The third allegation is that the Spitzbergen sea is more free from ice than any other part of the Arctic Regions. This statement is directly opposed to the evidence of every navigator who has ever reached the edge of the pack on those meridians. They have all, without a single exception, found an impenetrable barrier of ice between Greenland and Spitzbergen, and to the north of that group. The fourth is that the drift ice to the north of Spitzbergen offers just as much or as little impediment to navigation as the ice in Baffin's Bay. When it is remembered that no vessel has ever penetrated through the ice-fields north of Spitzbergen, notwithstanding numerous attempts, while a fleet of whalers has annually got through the Baffin's Bay ice since 1817, an idea may be formed of the value of this assertion. The fifth argument is that the sea north of Spitzbergen will never be entirely frozen over, not even in winter, nor covered with solid ice fit for sledge travelling. This is really the strongest objection to the Spitzbergen route, for the constant movement of the ice away from land will make it impossible to winter in it, and most dangerous to enter it at all. The sixth assertion is that from Sir Edward Parry's farthest point a navigable sea was extending, far away to the north; and that old Dutch skippers vowed they had sailed to 88° N., and beyond the Pole itself. The statement respecting Parry is the very reverse of the real fact. That officer, at his extreme point, found the ice thicker and the floes more extensive than any he had previously met with; and there was a strong yellow ice-blink always overspreading the northern horizon, showing that the Polar pack still stretched away to the northward. The argument derived from the old Dutch skippers may safely be left to shift for itself. The seventh point is, that the Polar region north of Spitz-

bergen consists of sea and not land. This is a mere assumption ;
but, if correct, it is the very reason that the Spitzbergen route is
the worst that could be selected. The eighth argument is that
Parry's expedition occupied six months, a circumstance which can
only have weight with those who prefer a hasty and perfunctory
cruise to deliberate and careful exploration.

18. So much for the first letter. The second letter contains the
following argument. Dr. Petermann urges that there will be no
difficulty in boring through the Polar ice-fields north of 80°,
because Sir James Ross got through an extensive pack in the
Antarctic Regions in latitude 62°, after it had drifted and become
loose for many hundreds of miles over a boundless ocean. The
fallacy of this comparison was shown by Admiral Collinson * at
the time. Finally, Dr. Petermann asks for any reason, however
slight, why it would not be as easy to sail from Spitzbergen to
the Pole and back as to go up Baffin's Bay to the entrance of
Smith Sound. The reason is clear enough, and is well known to
all Arctic navigators. North of Spitzbergen any vessel pushing
into the ice is at the mercy of the drifting floes and fields. In
Baffin's Bay there is land ice, along which a vessel can make
progress while the pack drifts past. The consequence is, that
while a fleet of whalers passes up Baffin's Bay every year, no
vessel has ever penetrated through the pack north of Spitzbergen.

19. Such were Dr. Petermann's arguments. They had the effect
of delaying the resumption of Arctic research by the English for
ten years. For they were adopted by Admirals Belcher, Richards,
Ommanney, and Inglefield ; unanimity among Arctic authorities
was thus destroyed, and, in Osborn's absence, success was ob-
viously hopeless. I, nevertheless, prepared drafts of letters to
other scientific Societies, and a most encouraging reply was received from the Linnæan. I also drew up a letter to the First
Lord of the Admiralty, which was signed by Sir Roderick Murchison, and the Duke of Somerset received a deputation. His Grace,
however, naturally said that as Arctic authorities differed as to the
route, the Admiralty could not decide that question ; and that it
would be better to wait for the result of the Swedish Expedition,
which was then about to be sent to Spitzbergen.

20. It only remained to watch for another favourable opportunity
of re-opening the question. But Sherard Osborn, on his return from
India in 1866, did not relax his efforts. Every endeavour was
made to interest the general public in Arctic work, and, under
Osborn's inspiration, I wrote an article in the 'Quarterly Review'

* 'R. G. S. Proceedings,' ix. p. 118.

for July 1865, and several reviews and articles on the subject
between 1866 and 1871. Papers were also prepared and read at
the annual meetings of the British Association in 1865 and
1866.

21. At last Sherard Osborn decided that the time had arrived for
a formal renewal of his proposal; and at a meeting of the Geographical Society on April 22nd, 1872, he read his second paper on
the exploration of the North Polar area. The great point now was
to secure unanimity among Arctic authorities, before approach-
ing the Government on the subject: and the paper was mainly
intended to review the work of Swedes, Germans, and Austrians in
the Spitzbergen direction since 1865; and to show that the theory
maintained in Dr. Petermann's letters was in opposition to the
practical experience of recent explorers. Those explorers had
spoken with no uncertain voice. For instance, M. Nordenskiöld
said that " the field of drift ice to the north of Spitzbergen consists of ice so closely packed together that even a boat cannot force
its way between the pieces, still less a vessel, though propelled by
steam. All experience seems to prove that the Polar basin, when
not covered with compact unbroken ice, is filled with closely-
packed unnavigable drift in which, during certain very favourable
years, some large apertures may be found, which apertures, however, do not extend very far to the north." Osborn quoted Nordenskiöld, Koldewey, and Payer as practical men; and again urged
the adoption of the route by Smith Sound. On this occasion Sir
Henry Rawlinson, then President of the Geographical Society,
advocated the resumption of Arctic discovery, and ever afterwards not only co-operated with Osborn, but took a leading
and active part in furthering the cause. Dr. Hooker and Dr.
Carpenter dwelt upon the valuable scientific results of Arctic
research. Sir George Back again warmly supported Osborn's
views; and Admiral Richards, who had at the former meeting
opposed the movement, now gave in his adhesion to it.

22. I then drafted a Report for the adoption of a Committee appointed by the Council of the Geographical Society to consider the
best means of bringing the subject before the Government: consisting of Sir George Back, Admiral Collinson, Admiral Ommanney,
Admiral Richards, Sir Leopold McClintock, Captain Sherard
Osborn, Dr. Rae, Mr. Findlay, and myself.

23. In this Report the three canons of Arctic exploration were
repeated, the various scientific results were enumerated in detail,
and all mention of reaching the North Pole as an object, was purposely excluded. The Smith Sound route was recommended as

the best for exploring new coast-lines, and thus increasing geographical knowledge. The Report was unanimously adopted by all the members of the Committee, and also by the Council of the Society, on the 29th of April, 1872.

24. In July 1872 I began the work of editing the 'Geographical Magazine,' and my first number opened with an article by Sherard Osborn, on the renewal of Arctic discovery. In the same number I commenced the publication of the 'Threshold of the Unknown Region,' which was continued monthly until March 1873, and published as a separate volume in July 1873. The plan of this work had been conceived, and the greater part was written in 1865, but it was not then published. The second edition rapidly followed the first, the third edition appeared in January 1875, and the fourth in December 1875. The success of this little work proved the great change in public opinion which had taken place since 1865. A healthy interest in the glorious achievements of the Arctic worthies of former days was taking the place of sneering indifference, and Englishmen were once more becoming alive to the importance of maritime enterprise.

25. In August 1872 a paper on the renewal of Arctic research, by Sherard Osborn, was read at the meeting of the British Association at Brighton.

26. On December 16th, 1872, Sir Henry Rawlinson and Sherard Osborn, accompanied by Dr. Hooker and a large deputation, had an interview with Mr. Lowe and Mr. Goschen, to urge the importance of despatching an Arctic Expedition; and the whole matter was fully explained both by Sir Henry and by Osborn. But the reply was unsatisfactory.

27. Official doubts were, however, on the eve of being overcome. All classes of the people, thanks to Osborn's exertions, were beginning to unite with men of science in the desire that the tradition of Arctic discovery should be preserved and handed down to posterity; and that Englishmen should not abandon that career of noble adventure which has done so much to form the national character, and to give our country the rank she still maintains. The interest, once very keenly felt in such enterprises, was rapidly being revived.

28. The year 1873 was one of much activity. On the 10th of February I read a paper, at a meeting of our Society, on recent discoveries east of Spitzbergen and on attempts to reach the Pole on the Spitzbergen meridians, in which it was shown that the best route for the objects which the Society had in view, was by Smith Sound. On that occasion Sir Henry Rawlinson declared that the

Society would recommend and promote the despatch of an expedition by way of Smith Sound, because by that route the widest extent of coast line would be discovered and explored, and the most important scientific results obtained.

29. The goal was now in view. A few more well-conceived efforts, and success was secured. Osborn found that the objection to which official and other persons most obstinately clung was based on the supposed dangers and difficulties of ice navigation. He, therefore, came to the conclusion that nothing would tend more to dispel this objection than some practical proof or trial, and that it was desirable that a naval officer should proceed to the Arctic Regions in a whaler, and return with a full report of all he had seen and experienced. He selected for this service Commander A. H. Markham, who had been a volunteer since the question was first raised in 1865; and who now made a cruise with Captain Adams in the whaler 'Arctic' from May to August 1873. The publication of his narrative in 1874, 'A Whaling Cruise in Baffin's Bay and the Gulf of Boothia, with an Introduction by Rear-Admiral Sherard Osborn, C.B.,' the second edition of which appeared in 1875, was another means of exciting public interest in Arctic work.

30. In the spring of 1873, a joint Committee of the Royal and Royal Geographical Societies was appointed to prepare an exhaustive Memorandum on the scientific results to be derived from Arctic exploration, and on the reasons why such researches can best be accomplished by a naval expedition despatched under Government auspices. The Committee was composed of the same members as sat on the Arctic Committee of 1872 for the Geographical Society, and of Dr. Hooker, Mr. Busk, Mr. Prestwich, Dr. Carpenter, Dr. Allman, Mr. Evans, General Strachey, and Mr. Fergusson for the Royal Society. In this Memorandum, dated June 1873, which was widely distributed, the scientific results were fully discussed in a series of paragraphs furnished by Dr. Hooker, Professor Allman, Mr. Prestwich, General Strachey, and Professor Newton; while the arguments derived from former experience and general policy were by Sherard Osborn. With these materials I drew up the Memorandum, which was unanimously adopted by the Joint Committee, and also by our Council. In this manifesto, as in that of 1872, the object was declared to be the exploration of as large an area as possible of the unknown region; while all allusion to attaining the highest northern latitude possible, or reaching the Pole, was again purposely omitted.

31. In August 1873 I read a paper on the importance of Arctic exploration, at the meeting of the British Association at Bradford;

and in the following October I contributed an article on the same subject to the ' Contemporary Review.'

32. The year 1874 was destined to see the complete success of the efforts of Sherard Osborn and those who had worked with him for the previous ten years. The Society, which had approved and encouraged these efforts, thus has the honour of having initiated, steadily and perseveringly advocated, and finally of having secured the adoption of a measure of great importance for the advancement of geographical knowledge.

33. On the 1st of August, 1874, Sir Henry Rawlinson and Admiral Sherard Osborn, accompanied by Dr. Hooker, had a very satisfactory interview with Mr. Disraeli, and on the 17th of November the Prime Minister addressed a letter to Sir Henry Rawlinson announcing that Her Majesty's Government had determined to lose no time in organizing a suitable expedition; the two objects being the exploration of the region round the North Pole, and the encouragement of maritime enterprise.

34. The further measures connected with the equipment, and the instructions, then passed into the hands of the Admiralty. Two vessels were selected and prepared for ice navigation, and officers and men were appointed between November 1874 and February 1875.

35. It is important that the objects of the Geographical Society, and the rules based on experience which guided us in our recommendations, should be kept in mind. The Council, in all its memoranda, discarded the attainment of the highest possible northern latitude and an attempt to reach the North Pole as useful objects. Such aims, by themselves, were considered to be devoid of interest as of utility. Our objects were to explore the largest area possible of the unknown region, from a fixed base of operations, in order to secure useful scientific results. The Council, also, since 1872, by the unanimous advice of its Arctic Committees, discarded the Spitzbergen route, including an attempt to push into the Polar pack away from the land. The course advocated was to navigate along a coast line, to include the passing of at least one Arctic winter in the scheme, and to look to sledge travelling as the main instrument of discovery and exploration. Consequently the Smith Sound route was, for the attainment of the above objects in accordance with these rules, the best that could be selected.

36. Such were the views of the Royal Geographical Society, of the Royal Society, and also of Her Majesty's Government as expressed in Mr. Disraeli's letter to Sir Henry Rawlinson. But the Admiralty thought fit to look upon them as secondary, and to make the

attainment of the highest possible northern latitude the main object of the Expedition. This deviation from the recommendations of the learned Societies was first announced by Admiral Richards, in a paper " On the Route towards the Pole for the Arctic Expedition of 1875," which was read at a meeting of the Geographical Society, presided over by the Prince of Wales, on February 8, 1875; but he added that the success of the Expedition did not depend on reaching the Pole, or even a very high northern latitude. In the discussion which followed, I took the opportunity of repeating the views of the Geographical Society that the work of the Arctic Expedition should be to explore as large an area as possible of the unknown region; and that, if the Pole was reached, the value of that achievement would consist in what was observed during the march, not in arriving at the Pole, which is a mere point without length, breadth, or thickness, and therefore of no possible interest to geographers.

37. The Instructions of the Admiralty to Captain Nares, as Commander of the Arctic Expedition, thus deviated from the objects and recommendations of our Society. The scope and primary object of the Expedition was declared to be to attain the highest northern latitude, and if possible to reach the North Pole. The work of exploration, which should have been the sole object, was mentioned as merely a secondary consideration. At the same time it was pointed out (in paragraph 15) that, in the absence of continuous land, sledge travelling over an unenclosed frozen sea for any considerable distance has never been found practicable. Thus the main object of the Expedition, in the view of the Admiralty, could not be attained unless the land trended north. The idea that this was the case appears to have been based on an erroneous American chart, on which a coast line, never seen, is shown to extend far to the north from Robeson Channel. But a very little inquiry would have shown the Admiralty that such a coast line did not exist, and indeed they could have obtained that information from Dr. Bessels, who was on board the ' Polaris.'

38. The objects of the Admiralty and of our Society would be the same if the land trended north. But if, as was found to be the case, it trended east and west, those objects would be antagonistic. While the main object of the Admiralty could only be very partially attained by sending a forlorn hope over the frozen sea on a useless and aimless quest, and exposed to great danger; those of our Society were fully secured by exploring the coast lines to the east and west.

39. In spite of these instructions, it was, however, pretty certain

that the Geographical Society's objects would be secured. The Expedition was to proceed by the route recommended by its Council, the advanced ship was, if possible, to cross the threshold of the unknown region, and winter in a position beyond any point reached by former discoverers, and exploration was to be conducted over the unknown area from this base of operations, with a view to securing those valuable scientific results enumerated in our Memoranda, though only as a secondary object.

40. Thus in reality the Arctic Expedition was an enterprise originated by the Geographical Society, and, on the whole, conducted in accordance with the rules and for the objects consistently and perseveringly advocated by its Council. These facts were fully and cordially recognized by Captain Nares before he started. The officers of the Expedition were entertained at dinner by the Geographical Club, and they received a hearty God-speed from the President, Council, and Fellows of the Royal Geographical Society before they sailed from Portsmouth on the 29th of May, 1875. But the great work of exploring the North Polar region could only be accomplished gradually; and it was never expected from the Smith Sound Expedition that it would do more than explore as large a portion of that region as was accessible from its base of operations with the means at its disposal.

II.

SUCCESSFUL RESULTS OF THE ARCTIC EXPEDITION OF 1875-76.

41. THE Arctic Expedition returned in October 1876, after having succeeded in crossing the threshold of the unknown region by the Smith Sound route, established a base of operations beyond it, and explored the unknown area from the base to the utmost extent possible with the means at their disposal. As far as the objects of the Admiralty were concerned, the 'Alert' had reached the highest north latitude ever attained by any ship, she had wintered farther north than any ship had ever wintered before, and Captain Markham had reached 83° 20′ 26″ N., a point nearer the North Pole than any human being had ever been before.

42. As regards the objects of the Geographical Society, namely, geographical discovery and research, the results of the Arctic Expedition are recorded in the Report of Sir George Nares, in the

two papers he has read at meetings of the Society, on December 12th, 1876, and March 26th, 1877, and in the Sledging Journals presented to Parliament. It is necessary to pass these results in review, before proceeding to consider the next step in advance that should be advocated, now that the work by the Smith Sound route is completed.

43. It was found that the coast lines beyond Robeson Channel trended away to west and north-east, forming the shores of a frozen Polar sea, and from the base of operations formed by the 'Alert' in 82° 27' N. the members of the Expedition examined the coasts for a distance of 300 miles. Along the whole of this distance the ice of the Polar sea was of the same character. Its existence was an unexpected and important discovery.

44. This ice was found to be from 80 to 100 feet in thickness, formed by continual additions from above (due to the annual snow-falls), which, by the increasing superincumbent weight, is gradually converted into snow-ice. Complete sections of the huge masses forced upon the shore were carefully taken, and they show the way in which the whole is formed, as well as its great age. These masses had been broken off from the large floes of ice, and were grounded in from four to ten fathoms along the whole coast. The process of formation of the ancient floes resembles that of glaciers, and the masses thus grounded had been chipped off from them. They in no way resemble the mere piles of broken-up hummocks that are often found on other Arctic shores. They are, in fact, icebergs broken off from fragments of floating glaciers, and have, therefore, received the appropriate name of FLOE-BERGS.

45. The 'Alert,' in September 1875, had thus reached an impenetrable sea of ancient ice intervening between those lonely shores and the North Pole. It is not, however, one vast congealed mass never in motion, which would have been the case if it had been formed in a stagnant and confined sea. On the contrary, it is subjected to annual disruption, and to violent commotion during the summer months. Early in July the whole mass is in motion, driving backwards and forwards with the winds and currents, its main course being towards the east. The floes grind against each other and are broken in fragments, while, whenever the angular corners of any of the fields meet, there pools of water are formed. In September the frost sets in, and these pools and narrow lanes are frozen over with ice that becomes about six feet thick during the winter, but motion still continues, and ridges of hummocks are thrown up between the floes. The stillness of the Polar winter does not prevail until late in October or November. Then a new

formation of ice commences, and goes on for seven months, which far more than counterbalances the decay during the summer.

46. Captain Markham's memorable journey away from the land from April to June 1876, directly across the frozen Polar sea, gave further opportunities of studying its character. It was found to consist of very small and rugged floes, separated by ranges of ice hummocks from 30 to 50 feet high and sometimes a quarter of a mile wide, while the occasional streams of young ice at the foot of the hummocks were narrow and of small extent. The hummock ridges consisted of a vast collection of débris of the previous summer's broken-up pack ice, which had been refrozen during the winter into one chaotic rugged mass of angular blocks of every possible shape. The intermediate floes of ancient ice were very rugged, and, on Captain Markham's route, never as much as a mile wide. The largest floe that was seen was farther to the eastward, blocking up the opening of Robeson Channel, and was several miles in extent. The surfaces of the floes were studded over with rounded, blue-topped ice humps from 10 to 20 feet high, the depressions between them being filled with snow deeply scored into ridges by the prevailing wind.

47. Such is the nature of the great Polar sea beyond the channels leading from Smith Sound, which was discovered by the Arctic Expedition of 1875–76. It is so totally different from the Polar pack met with north of Spitzbergen, that, with a view to that precision without which physical geography cannot make progress as a science, it was necessary that some distinctive term should be applied to it. This portion of the Polar ocean was, therefore, named the PALÆOCRYSTIC SEA, or sea of ancient ice: a name which has now been adopted by geographers both in England and on the Continent.

48. Careful and diligent observation furnished some *data* by which a judgment might be formed of the probable extent of the Palæocrystic Sea. It is certain that land was not near to the north, because hills were ascended to a height of 2500 feet and upwards on clear days, and there was not a sign of land. But there are other considerations all tending to the same conclusion. There are no flights of birds to the north, which certainly would be the case if there was land; and the only living thing that was seen on the Palæocrystic Sea, by the northern division of sledges, was a little snow bunting that had strayed from the nearest shore. Further evidence is furnished by the fact that animal marine life almost ceases to exist in the ice-covered Polar sea. The cold currents destroy whales' food, and there are no cetaceans. Except

one or two stragglers, no seals were seen, consequently there were
no bears ; and no human beings have ever before trodden the
shores of the Palæocrystic Sea. For the Eskimos, like the bears,
depend on seals for their means of subsistence, and all traces of
them, therefore, cease with the seals and bears, where the palæocrystic floes commence. The falcons, which prey on marine life,
also entirely cease.

49. It is remarkable, however, that the Arctic land animals, both
mammals and birds, are found up to the most northern point
in 83° N., though in much smaller numbers than at Melville
Island, and in other localities in the Arctic Regions farther south.
Musk oxen were found, and the wolves which always follow
them. Foxes and many little lemmings followed by the great
snowy owls that prey upon them ; the musk oxen and lemmings
both living on the purple saxifrage. There were also hares,
ptarmigan, brent geese, knots, turnstones, and the few birds
living on the small fresh-water lakes. But here they all ended,
and no birds took their flights to the northward. The Palæocrystic Sea is a sea of solitude.

50. The great extent of this Polar ocean is assumed on the above
grounds. There is also evidence that it is a comparatively shallow
sea. The northern division of sledges, at a distance of forty miles
from the land, found bottom in only 72 fathoms ; and between
that point and the shore several huge floe-bergs were observed,
apparently rising out of the centres of floes, which were probably
aground. Another indication of the present shallowness of the
Polar sea is the general recent upheaval of the adjacent land.
Drift wood was found far above any point to which it could have
been carried by ice or water.

51. The shore of the Palæocrystic Sea to the westward, after cul-
minating at Cape Colombia, trends away south of west ;' and it was
deduced, from similarity of tides, direction of prevailing winds,
and movements of the ice, that this trend continued south-west-
ward towards Prince Patrick Island. Similar evidence as regards
the drift of the ice, and the comparison of winds with those
experienced by the ' Germania' on the east coast of Greenland, led
to the belief that the north coast, from the farthest point discovered by Commander Beaumont, also trended south to Cape
Bismarck. A study of tides by Professor Haughton confirms this
view.

52. As regards the distribution of land and sea within the unknown area, and its general hydrography, the discoveries of the
Expedition are important. And it usually happens that when a new

geographical fact is revealed, through the labours of scientific explorers, it is found that it harmonizes with other isolated pieces of knowledge which previously stood alone as it were, and were not intelligible without it. Thus the value of discoveries is scarcely ever confined to the work itself; but they throw light upon the true bearings of former work, and help towards the elucidation of far larger questions. As regards the Palæocrystic Sea discovered by the late Arctic Expedition, this is eminently the case.

53. Referring to the information gathered by former explorers, we find that Captain Collinson, in coasting along the Arctic shore of North America, discovered that similar ancient ice composed the pack bounding the lane of open water along which he was able to pass to the westward in the 'Enterprise' in 1851. When he wintered in Camden Bay in 1853–54, he made an attempt to examine this ancient ice by sledging, but he was stopped on the second day by masses of broken-up hummocks and heavy uneven floes; in short, by obstacles similar to those which were encountered by the northern division of sledges in 1876. In 1850 Captain M'Clure, in the 'Investigator,' actually ran up a lane of water leading into this pack, and had gone some distance before he ascertained the fearful nature of the ice on either side of him. He then made all haste to escape from it. The same ancient ice extends along the whole western side of Banks Island; and the 'Investigator,' in daily and hourly peril of destruction, passed along between it and the cliffs, in the navigating season of 1851. The surfaces of the floes are described as resembling rolling hills, some of them a hundred feet from base to summit. Sherard Osborn describes this pack as " aged sea ice, which may be centuries old, and it seems, from the want of outlets, likely to increase yet in thickness to an unlimited degree ; the accumulated action of repeated thaws, and the almost constant fall of snow on the upper surface, giving it a peculiar hill and dale appearance." M'Clure, in one of his notices, warned those who might find it that if his vessel got into this pack she would never be heard of again, and should not be followed.

54. Mecham found the same ancient ice along the western shore of Prince Patrick Island in 1853. He describes it as " tremendous," and he came to the conclusion that the sea on which it floats was of great extent. He adds that " the character and appearance of the pack driven against the land, and in every direction to seaward, thoroughly convinced him of the impossibility of penetrating with ships to the southward and westward, against such impediments." Here then was again the Palæocrystic Sea.

55. Standing by itself, as an isolated geographical fact, the heavy ice seen by Collinson, M'Clure, and Mecham failed to reveal the whole truth. With the above data alone before him, Sherard Osborn saw at once that no one who had penetrated elsewhere into the Arctic Regions had ever met with similar oceanic ice. He described it as a vast floating glacier-like mass, surging to and fro in an enclosed area, bounded on the south by the shores of North America, on the west by Wrangell Land, and on the east by Banks and Prince Patrick islands. But where was the boundary to the north? Here Sherard Osborn needed the *data* furnished by the recent discoveries to guide him. In their absence he came to the conclusion, which was perfectly justified by the materials actually before him, that the ancient ice was formed in a land-locked sea, and that it was bounded to the north by land continuing west from Prince Patrick's Island.*

56. The discoveries of the Arctic Expedition of 1875–76 have thrown light upon and explained all these interesting questions. We now know that the Palæocrystic Sea extends from the shores of North America to the north coast of Greenland, a distance of 1200 miles: for the gap of 400 miles which is still unexplored between Prince Patrick Island and the most western point reached by the Expedition, is a continuation of coast line or island, as is deduced from coincidences of winds, tide, and drift. The sea is also shown to be of great width, in short, a Polar ocean of vast extent.

57. Dr. Petermann† has recently endeavoured to explain these facts on the same principle as that adopted by Admiral Sherard Osborn, namely, that the Palæocrystic Sea is practically stagnant, and confined on all sides by land. Osborn, from the data then before him, supposed the frozen sea off Banks Island to be of comparatively small extent, and that it was bounded to the north by a continuation of the Parry Islands. Dr. Petermann, in the light of the new discoveries, recognizes the existence of a vast Palæocrystic Sea of far greater extent than Osborn supposed; but he also would confine it by hypothetical land extending from Greenland across the Pole to Siberia. But Osborn had grounds for his theory, which Petermann had not. The former authority had gathered from the officers of the 'Investigator' that the ice was comparatively motionless, that it never went more than a few miles off the American coast, leaving a narrow belt of water, and that, directly the gale ceased, it surged back again with its edge grounded in 100 feet of water. We now know that this is only partially

* See ' Threshold of the Unknown Region ' (4th ed.), pp. 188-195.
† ' Macmillau's Magazine.'

correct, and that in portions of the Palæocrystic Sea there is a drift to the east, although little of the ancient ice finds a means of escape. But Dr. Petermann's theory. is dependent upon the stagnancy of a vast ocean, and militates against the deductions respecting the insularity of Greenland, based on a study of the tides.

58. The knowledge of the existence of the Palæocrystic Sea, due to the discoveries of the late Expedition, added to the discovery of Franz Josef Land by the Austrians, and to the German observations on the east coast of Greenland, enable us to comprehend, with a nearer approach to accuracy, the general relations of the Polar area to the rest of the world as regards the circulation of water and the distribution of land and sea. The drift eastward of the ice north of Grant Land seems to be due to the great flow of warmer water into the Polar area, which, as a cold current, seeks an outlet southward at every opening, owing to the Polar area itself being surcharged. The warmer water, flowing up between Greenland and Spitzbergen as a submarine current, appears to come to the surface along the Siberian coast, and, aided by the discharged volume from the rivers, it causes a current round the area from left to right, and also across from the eastern to the western hemisphere. Hence, probably, the tremendous pressure on Grant Land and the north shore of Greenland, as well as the drift eastward. But there is much yet to learn.

59. The geographical and hydrographical results of the Arctic Expedition are the most important, because they have a practical bearing on the general system of oceanic currents and of meteorology, and consequently form an essential part of a vast whole. Without a knowledge of the hydrography of the Polar Region, all the general theories of oceanic currents must be incomplete; and Arctic research is, therefore, necessary to a science which is of practical utility. But the Expedition brought home other results which are certainly not less interesting than those discoveries which immediately concern the Geographical Society. Among these may be mentioned the examination into the geological formation of the whole coast line on the west side of the Smith Sound channels from Cape Isabella to Cape Union, as well as of the shores of the Palæocrystic Sea on either side of Robeson Channel. Collections of rocks and fossils were made at every point, including a very complete Upper Silurian series, and the mountain limestone shells and corals of Cape Joseph Henry. But by far the most important geological discovery was that relating to the existence of tertiary coal in 82° N., and the former extension of miocene vegeta-

tion to that parallel. The Expedition also made an exhaustive
collection of the biology of a region previously almost entirely
unknown to science : the region north of the 82nd parallel, as distinguished from the Arctic countries to the southward.   The
whole *flora* of the new region has been brought home ; and it must
be remembered that meagre though this *flora* certainly is, Dr.
Hooker has shown that it possesses special interest ; in connection
with the remarkable distribution of American and Scandinavian
plants.   The zoology of the newly discovered region has also
been exhaustively examined, and very complete collections made
as regards mammalia, birds, fishes, insects, molluscs, crustacea,
echinoderms, and a vast number of microscopic forms.   In physics
a complete series of meteorological, magnetic, tidal and other
observations, covering a year, has been taken at two stations.

60. I now turn to the conduct and management of the Expedition which secured these valuable results.   Consisting of two
steamers admirably officered and manned, it had an advantage over
former expeditions composed of sailing vessels towed by steam
tenders.   But, on the other hand, it suffered from several disadvantages ; as compared with the two last expeditions employed
in the search for Franklin.   The sledge equipments and the
clothing were identical, and the provisions (with the exception of
the salt beef, which was very bad in the late Expedition) were
equally good ; but it appears to have been impracticable to fit a
steamer with the warming apparatus which was so conducive to
health and comfort in former voyages.   Another serious dis-
advantage in 1876 was the numerical weakness of the late, as
compared with the two previous expeditions under Austin and
Belcher.   While the latter had an effective force of one hundred
and eighty men, the work of the late Expedition was necessarily
more restricted, owing to its being seriously under-manned in
comparison.   It only had one hundred and twenty men, including
chaplains.

61. The most essential object in the conduct of an Arctic
Expedition, and the crucial test of its success, is the crossing of
the threshold of the unknown region, and the attainment of a
position as a base of operations beyond any hitherto discovered.
If this is achieved, success is certain.   It may be slight or important ; but some measure of success is certain, if a base of operations is established within the unknown region.   The navigation
of the channels leading north from Smith Sound is the most
difficult of any that has been experienced in Arctic coast waters,
and as soon as the Palæocrystic floes are met with north of the

c 2

82nd parallel, there is great and constant danger. To have brought a ship through all this, and to have found winter quarters on the open and exposed coast of the Palæocrystic Sea, protected only by grounded floe-bergs which might at any time be driven higher up or swept away, was in itself a great success. No other Arctic navigator ever forced his ships through such obstacles, and brought them safely back again ; and this establishment of a base of operations within the unknown region called forth all the highest qualities of a commander—incessant watchfulness, great presence of mind, rapid yet cautious decision, and consummate seamanship.

62. The next service to be performed was the laying out of depôts by autumn sledge travelling ; and in this the late Expedition excelled all that preceded it, whether the amount of work done, the duration of absence from the ship, or the special difficulties and hardships be considered.

63. Next to the establishment of a base of operations beyond any point previously reached, the most important preparation for exploration and discovery by sledges is the management of the Expedition during the long darkness of an Arctic winter, and the maintenance of the health and spirits of the men. The difficulties, in this respect, of the Expedition of 1875–76 were greater than any that had previously been encountered, because the winter was the longest and the most severe, and the continuous darkness was the most prolonged that had ever been endured in the Arctic Regions. Moreover, the absence of the warming apparatus supplied to former expeditions increased the difficulty of preserving health. When these special disadvantages are considered, the efforts of the commanding officers of the late Expedition to preserve the health and keep up the spirits of the men are deserving of high praise. Extemporized arrangements of various kinds provided for ventilation and washing, the greatest care was taken that the daily rations of lime juice were actually drunk, special attention was devoted to the enforcement of regular exercise and to diet, and the recreation and amusement of the men were kept up with a zest and energy which was never surpassed in any former expedition. The management during an Arctic winter of unparalleled length and severity was admirable in all respects.

64. When the sun returned, the scheme for exploration by sledges was matured ; and early in April 1876, under difficulties and exposed to an extremity of cold beyond anything that had been experienced in former expeditions, the sledging parties left the ships.

65. Owing to the Admiralty Instructions, it was incumbent

upon Captain Nares to push his principal party due north over the Palæocrystic Sea, with the object of attaining the highest possible northern latitude. As there was no land, it was not possible to lay out depôts, and all supplies, together with boats, had to be dragged on the sledges. The Admiralty had impressed upon Captain Nares (*para.* 15 *of Instructions*) that, in the absence of continuous land, sledge travelling for any considerable distance has never been found practicable. Yet in order to attain the main object of the Admiralty, the attempt had to be made. The farthest north hitherto reached was on July 23rd, 1827, when Parry got to 82° 45′ N. But this was during the summer, and the work was done without the endurance of serious hardships, although the weights to be dragged per man were very great, namely 268 lbs. Captain Markham won the palm from Parry after he had held it for nearly forty-nine years. On May 12th, 1876, he reached 83° 20′ 26″ N., in the face of hardships and difficulties without a parallel in the annals of Arctic sledge travelling. Thus gallantly and successfully were the Admiralty Instructions complied with by reaching the highest northern point ever attained by man.

66. Three other extended sledge parties were organized to secure the true objects of the Expedition, from the point of view of the Geographical Society, namely, the extension of geographical knowledge. One was to explore the unknown region to the westward of the base of operations to the farthest point attainable; the second was to press eastward along the northern coast of Greenland; and the third was to examine the deep inlet named after Lady Franklin, which was believed to be a strait. All did their work admirably, and extended their explorations to the utmost limit, in two sad cases beyond the utmost limit of human endurance. They fully, completely, and with heroic self-devotion, fulfilled the objects of the Geographical Society, by exploring that portion of the unknown region accessible by the Smith Sound route to the farthest extent possible with the means at their disposal.

67. The only competent judges of their work, from the point of view of actual experience in sledge travelling, are the officers who served in former expeditions; and it is, therefore, desirable to quote here the opinion of Captain R. V. Hamilton, R.N., C.B., who served in the Arctic Expeditions of 1850–51 and 1852–54, and commanded sledges during three seasons. His evidence is as follows:—" I have no hesitation in expressing my admiration for the zeal, energy, and brave determination of Commander Markham

and Lieutenant Beaumont and their crews to overcome the un-precedented obstacles they encountered—in my opinion very far greater than any previous sledge parties have experienced. The journeys were extended to the utmost limits of safety—prudence would have dictated an earlier return, not doing so is the only fault (if a fault) committed. No officer could have pushed on so far unless thoroughly supported by his crew; no crew would have so supported their officer had he not shown he exacted nothing from them he did not perform. Lieutenant Aldrich does not appear to have encountered, except from soft snow, greater obstacles than previous parties of the 'Assistance' and 'Resolute.' Had his men been in as good health as ours were, I believe his average distance would have been little less than my own in 1853 after a previous spring's experience of travelling. When the scurvy prostrated most of the crew, they displayed equal courage and patience under trial as the other parties. Till I read these journals, I had an impression on my mind *we* would have done better; but no unbiassed person can read these modest, unassuming narratives and retain that impression."* I cannot refrain from adding the verdict of an able writer in the 'Quarterly Review,' which expresses the opinion of every true Englishman on this subject. "Surely nothing finer was ever recorded than this advance of three sledges, one to the north, another to the east, a third to the west, laden down with sick and dying men, in obedience to an order to do their best in their separate directions. And nothing more touching was ever penned than the narratives, full of tenderness and simplicity, in which the sailor-writers tell their story. These gallant seamen have failed to reach the Pole, but they have won a proud place in their country's annals. They have done Englishmen good."†

68. The unprecedented and most unexpected outbreak of scurvy both among the men and officers who remained on board, and among the sledge travellers, was a calamity, which enhances our admiration of the amount of useful work actually accomplished by the Arctic Expedition of 1875-76. The exciting cause of scurvy is very generally believed to be the absence of fresh vegetables, and this exciting cause existed in all previous Arctic Expeditions exactly in the same measure as in that of 1875-76. The pre-disposing causes are all conditions inimical to health which exist during an Arctic winter, including intense cold, long darkness, absence of fresh provisions, damp, and confined air. These also

---

* Evidence before the Scurvy Committee; Question No. 3091.
† 'Quarterly Review,' January 1877; Art. v. p. 185.

existed in former expeditions when scurvy did not appear, but never during anything like the same length of time. It was undoubtedly the prolonged duration of these predisposing causes which produced the outbreak.

69. But this could not possibly have been foreseen. At the end of the winter the medical officers believed all the sledge travellers to be in perfect health; and consequently, in arranging their dietary, Captain Nares was fully justified in the assumption that the conditions were identical with those existing in previous expeditions, and in following the best former precedents. Accordingly he adopted the scale of diet, including preserved potatoes as an antiscorbutic, but not including lime juice, which long experience had shown to be the best. It was exactly the same scale as had been used in former expeditions and as was recommended by Sir Leopold McClintock, except that the allowance of rum was decreased by one half, and that of tea proportionally increased. No sledge parties had ever before been disabled by scurvy, and none had ever taken lime juice as a daily ration. Hence there is no mention of scurvy and no allusion to precautions against it, in the instructions drawn up for the guidance of former sledge travellers, by the Arctic medical officers. The lime juice was supplied in jars and bottles, and the contents of each bottle become solid masses in an Arctic April, which cannot be used until thoroughly thawed and re-mixed.* This would entail the use of additional fuel, and a serious increase of the weight to be dragged on the sledges. But the great objection to the daily thawing of rations of lime juice is the additional hardship and misery it would cause. No one who has not travelled during April in the Arctic Regions can have any idea of the sufferings it entails, especially upon the cook, and of the importance of doing nothing to increase that suffering, after a long day of intense toil.

70. These were the reasons why daily rations of lime juice were not included in the sledge dietary by Captain Nares; and, from the point of view of the experience and information before him, and from which he had to form his decision, he was undoubtedly right. It is, I believe, the unanimous opinion of all Arctic sledge travellers that Captain Nares did not commit an error of judgment on this point, and that he had no reason to deviate from the lessons of former experience.

* In an experiment at Netley the lime juice is reported to have frozen homogeneously. In the Arctic Regions this is not the case. The component parts are separated in the freezing process, owing probably to its much greater rapidity; and the whole volume must consequently be thawed and re-mixed every time it is used.

71. It has been alleged that he received instructions to issue daily rations of lime juice to the sledge travellers, from the Medical Director-General, Sir A. Armstrong. This is not the case. He was furnished with a memorandum of hints and suggestions by the Director-General simply for his information, but not for his guidance, and they were not instructions. He was also furnished with similar hints by another equally high Arctic medical authority, in which no such advice was given. The decision was properly left entirely to his own discretion. The suggestion of Dr. Armstrong was in opposition to all former practice and experience, and consequently, if its adoption was considered indispensable by that official, he ought to have given Captain Nares some reason for deviating from former precedents. Above all, he ought to have suggested means of using the lime juice while travelling in April; for unless this was done the mere advice to drag it on the sledges was useless. It now appears that lime juice can be taken in lozenges, in biscuit, or in the pemican; but this ought to have been thought of by those who considered its use indispensable to sledging parties, before the Expedition sailed.

72. The unexpected outbreak of scurvy was the one single calamity in an otherwise successful expedition. As soon as it was known, every precaution was taken to check its progress, and, thanks to the skill and untiring watchful care of the senior medical officer, there was not a single man on the sick list when the ships arrived at Portsmouth. All sledge parties which went away in the warmer months were of course supplied with daily rations of lime juice, and the fact that scurvy nevertheless broke out, seems to be a conclusive proof that the original outbreak was not due to the want of lime juice on the sledges, but to causes which were in operation, though undetected, before the sledges started, causes due to the unparalleled duration of winter darkness.

73. The outbreak of scurvy, however, was not an unmixed evil. It has taught lessons which will be of great value hereafter, and the elaborate investigations of the Scurvy Committee ought to produce results which will be useful in the conduct of future Arctic Expeditions. Nor should the examples of heroism called forth by the terrible sufferings of the sledge travellers be overlooked. They have added to the prestige of our navy, and will have an enduring value. The Quarterly reviewer says most truly "they have done Englishmen good."

74. At the conclusion of the sledging season, in August 1876, Captain Nares was able to review the work that had been accomplished. The outbreak of scurvy had made it his imperative duty

to return to England, in order to avoid a certain and serious loss of life which would have been utterly unjustifiable. But even if perfect health had been happily maintained, it would have been his duty to return. For the work was done, and done thoroughly. As regards the objects of the Admiralty, the highest northern latitude ever attained by any human being had been reached, and it had been found impracticable to advance farther towards the Pole by the Smith Sound route. The exploring work desired by the Royal Geographical Society was satisfactorily completed. A point had been reached to the westward beyond which exploration would be better conducted by another route. To the eastward a point was attained beyond which further discovery must be made by the route on the east coast of Greenland. The true objects of the Expedition, namely, to explore that portion of the unknown Polar region which was accessible by the Smith Sound route, were fully secured. The nature of the ice in the Palæocrystic Sea, and of the newly-discovered coast lines, showed that this part of the Polar ocean was not navigable; and the officers of the late Expedition were forced to the same conclusions on this point as had formerly been arrived at by M'Clure and Mecham. Consequently it was the duty of Captain Nares to obey the order contained in the 18th paragraph of the Admiralty Instructions, namely, " to use his best endeavours to rejoin his consort in 1876, and to return to England, provided that the spring exploration has been reasonably successful." After overcoming the same difficulties and dangers in the return voyage as had been encountered in 1875, the Expedition returned to England in October 1876, and received that cordial and hearty reception which its great success, its valuable geographical and other results, and the admirable conduct of officers and men, had so fully earned for it. The numerous testimonies to its success from the highest English authorities might be open to a suspicion of partiality, and I therefore prefer to quote the calm and impartial verdict of Chief Justice Daly, the President of the American Geographical Society. It is that " by the geographer and man of science the voyage will be pronounced a most important and successful one."

75. There is one result of the late Expedition which, though mentioned last, is not the least important. It was one which I know was very near to the heart of Admiral Sherard Osborn, the originator and chief promoter of the Expedition. I allude to the creation of a new generation of Arctic experts. The older generation is fast passing away, and if it had not been replaced, the traditions of the work would have died out. Now we once more

have a supply of experienced ice navigators and sledge travellers, trained in the best school, where they have done their work right well, and who are willing and ready to face new dangers, and to win new laurels in the Polar seas.

76. Thus the first great step has been accomplished by the Royal Geographical Society. Arctic discovery has been revived, an Expedition has been despatched, has completed its work, and has returned with a valuable increase to geographical knowledge. It remains for the Society to consider the next step, and to take care that this one success shall not be a spasmodic effort, but the commencement of continuous work in the same direction, to be persevered in until it is complete.

III.

ROUTES FOR FUTURE ARCTIC EXPEDITIONS.

77. THE arguments for the continuance and completion of Polar discovery are the same as those for its renewal. If Her Majesty's Government considered that the encouragement of maritime enterprise, and the exploration of the Polar Region were objects of sufficient importance to justify the despatch of an Expedition, to commence that work in 1875; those objects still exist, and the arguments for continuing and completing the work are quite as strong in 1877 as they were in 1875. Indeed, the success of the Expedition of 1875–76, and the experience gained by it, give new strength to those arguments; while the recent discoveries add fresh interest to Arctic research, and give additional scientific importance to its completion.

78. The discovery of the Palæocrystic Sea, and of 300 miles of its desolate shores, has entirely altered preconceived ideas, and added materially to our knowledge of the polar area. But this increased knowledge is still very partial, and one of the most interesting objects of future research will be to ascertain the extent of the sea of ancient ice, and the laws which regulate its formation.

79. The knowledge acquired in 1875–76 fully confirms the accuracy of the rules based on long experience, and formulated by Sherard Osborn in 1865. The necessity for navigating along a

coast line in order to cross the threshold of the unknown region, has received additional confirmation, the valuable results brought home by Captain Nares could not have been secured without wintering in the ice, and the use of sledges for exploring and making discoveries has again been shown to be indispensable. It is, therefore, established that the rules which guided the Council of the Royal Geographical Society in selecting Smith Sound as the best route and in recommending the course to be pursued, must still be considered in full force as guides for the selection of the next best route, and for laying down the principles on which Polar research should be continued.

80. It is now more certain than ever that the course advocated in Dr. Petermann's letters of 1865, namely, that of attempting to enter the drifting pack north of Spitzbergen in a steamer, in the hope of reaching a very high latitude, must be finally discarded. In the first place the object is insufficient. None of the results desired from Arctic exploration would be obtained by a summer cruise of this kind, away from land, even if it was successful. In the second place all practical navigators who have undertaken scientific investigations in the Spitzbergen seas since 1865, including Nordenskiöld, Koldewey, Payer, and Lamont, have declared that it will not be successful; and the opinions of Dr. Petermann himself appear to have been modified since that date. I have already quoted the views, based on great local experience, of Professor Nordenskiöld.* Those of Lieutenant Payer entirely coincide. He holds that navigation in the frozen seas remote from the land, is far more dangerous than navigation along a coast line, that it is entirely dependent on accident, exposed to grave catastrophes, and without any definite goal. " All the unsuccessful attempts," he adds, " to penetrate northward from Spitzbergen, were made by expeditions whose course and termination resemble each other as one egg resembles another." Payer repeats what Sherard Osborn had urged since 1865, and what ought now to be accepted as an incontrovertible canon of ice-navigation. In the words of Sir Edward Parry, " experience has clearly shown that the navigation of the Polar seas can never be performed with any degree of certainty, without a continuity of land. It was only by watching the openings between the ice and the shore that our late progress to the westward was effected (in 1819), and had the land continued in the desired direction, there can be no question that we should have continued to advance, however slowly, towards the completion of our enterprise."

* See page 7.

81. We must, therefore, continue to be guided by those canons of Arctic exploration which Sherard Osborn has formulated. But it must be remembered that the Smith Sound route was the best by which the threshold of the unknown region could be approached. The work in that direction is now completed, and the next best route cannot of course offer the same chances of success and equal advantages. The difficulties will increase as the work approaches completion; but so will the glory of surmounting them.

82. Four routes now remain for future expeditions. I. The Jones Sound route, the work of which will be to connect North Lincoln with Aldrich's farthest, and to ascertain the limits of the Palæocrystic Sea in that direction. II. The East Greenland route, to connect Cape Bismarck with Beaumont's farthest, and so complete the discovery of Greenland. III. The route of Franz Josef Land, to explore the northern side of the country discovered by Payer; and IV. The North-east Passage, by which a knowledge of the sea north of Siberia will be completed, and Wrangell Land will be explored.

83. The two latter routes will probably be found the most difficult, and it is not likely that all the work in either of those directions could be completed by one expedition. Payer and Weyprecht only reached the land discovered by them in 1873, by dint of a long and involuntary drift in the ice. It might be reached by a fortunate and skilful attempt either by the north coast of Spitzbergen, or to the eastward, according to the season. If a winter harbour could be reached on the western shore of Franz Josef Land, discoveries of great interest would be made by sledging parties, and annual communication might be secured by forming depôts on Gilies Land and other islands probably intervening between North-east Land and Zichy Island. Franz Josef Land seems to be a part of the Spitzbergen group, rising out of the same shallow sea, with deeper water to the north. But the exploration of its northern face will be very interesting, and will throw much light on the physical geography of the still unknown portion of the polar area.

84. The North-east Passage is surrounded with a halo of romance. It was the first achievement attempted by our earliest Arctic worthies and by the Dutch, and is connected with the names of Willoughby and Chancellor, of Pet and Jackman, of Barents and Linschoten. In later times the labours of Lutke, Nordenskiöld, Gardiner, Wiggins, and the Norwegian walrus hunters have given fresh interest to its approaches; the journeys of Anjou

and Wrangell have shown the great geographical interest which attaches to the sea north of Siberia; while the admission of an indication of Wrangell Land on the charts has made its complete exploration a necessary work for the future.

85. Since 1869 the voyages of Norwegian fishers have overcome the obstacles on the threshold of the North-east Passage, which were insuperable to the early navigators. They have sailed round Novaya Zemlya, and have traversed the Kara Sea. The point is to select the right time, in the season, for an attempt to cross the Sea of Kara. It has now been established by M. Nordenskiöld and Captain Wiggins that a steamer may always calculate upon being able to reach the mouth of the Yenisei River in August. It remains to be seen whether navigation can be extended round Capes Taimyr and Chelyuskin to the northern shores of the New Siberian Islands. Russian vessels have never been able to get beyond the mouth of the Pyasina. But in 1843 Middendorf saw extensive open water from Cape Taimyr during the summer, and the observations of both Anjou and Wrangell tend to the conclusion that, if Cape Chelyuskin could be rounded, the Polar sea north of Siberia might be navigated as far as Wrangell Land. The difficulties of crossing the threshold of the unknown region, and reaching new ground by this route, will doubtless be formidable. Nevertheless, important discoveries will reward the future explorer who boldly and successfully advances northwards on this line. He will be in the rear of the ice-laden Polar sea discovered by the Expedition of Captain Nares, and will thus complete the solution of the questions in physical geography connected with it.

86. It is, however, the two first routes that I have mentioned which offer the greatest advantages, and most nearly comply with the conditions that have been laid down; namely, those by Jones Sound and by the east coast of Greenland. By both the navigation would be along coast lines, and by both there is a reasonable expectation of being able to establish a base of operations beyond the threshold of the unknown region. Discovered by Baffin in 1616, Jones Sound is said to have been penetrated by Captain Lee in the 'Prince of Wales' whaler in 1848, for a distance of 150 miles. In August 1851, Sherard Osborn went a short distance up Jones Sound in the 'Pioneer,' but was stopped by floes stretching across the strait, and it was also entered by Inglefield in the 'Phœnix' in 1853. In the spring of 1853, Sir Edward Belcher explored the north coast of Grinnell Land, which forms the southern side of Belcher Channel leading from Jones Sound. He

found open water streaked with sailing ice, and the northern coast or islands trending to N.E. The floes were acted upon by a strong tide, and had evidently been in motion during the previous autumn. Early in June the flights of birds indicated water holes to the north, probably caused by the passage of a strong tidal wave in an east and west direction. The geographical results of an expedition up Jones Sound and Belcher Channel would be the completion of discoveries thence to Aldrich's farthest, including the distribution of land and sea towards Prince Patrick Island, and the character of the region north of the Parry group. The attainment of a suitable base of operations for the sledging journeys is almost certain, so that some measure of success by the Jones Sound route may be relied upon.

87. But, with equal advantages as regards the chances of success, the East Greenland route offers geographical results of greater importance, namely, the completion of the discovery of that vast mass of glacier-bearing land. The northern known part of East Greenland was discovered by Henry Hudson on June 13th, 1607, who called it "Hold with Hope," and reported that "for aught we could see, it is like to be a good land and worth the seeing." This was in latitude 73° N. Van Keulen, on his chart, has "Land van Edam" in 77° 10' N., discovered in 1655; and another part of the coast, seen in 1670, marked "Land van Lambert." In June 1822, Scoresby forced his ship through the ice floes which encumber the east coast, and surveyed it from Gale Hamke's Bay in 75° southwards to 69° N., finding little difficulty in sailing along the channel close in shore. In the following year, also during the month of June, Captain Clavering in the 'Griper,' with Captain Sabine on board, attempted to press through the ice to the east coast of Greenland in 77° 30' N., but was stopped by an unbroken field sixty miles long. On August 2nd, he again entered the ice in 75° 30' N., and passed through sailing ice, along the margin of solid fields, to the south-west, at last succeeding in reaching the land. He laid down the coast line from 72° to 76° N., while Captain Sabine took his observations on Pendulum Island.

88. The German Expedition sailed from Bremen on June 15th, 1869, consisting of the 'Germania,' a little steamer of 140 tons, and with a crew of seventeen men, and the 'Hansa' storeship. The crew of the 'Hansa' demonstrated the existence of a southerly drift along the east coast during the winter, while the 'Germania,' following in Captain Clavering's footsteps, reached a latitude of 75° 30' N., and wintered at the Pendulum Islands in 74° 30' N. By the 5th of August the 'Germania' reached open water in shore,

but the ice appeared to be firm and without sign of breaking up, to the north of Shannon Island (74° 56' to 75° 26' N.). To the south there was much open water. From August 17th to September 13th an attempt was made to go farther north, but without success, the fields being closely packed against the land ice. In 1870 a sledging journey (two sledges and ten men) was undertaken to the northward, between March 8th and April 27th, the first twenty-three days outwards taking the party to 77° N., the most northerly point ever reached on the east coast. Nothing but want of provisions (for they had no system of depôts) prevented a much further extension of the journey to the northward.

89. The opinion of the German explorers is unfavourable to the possibility of pushing much farther north along the east coast. But all depends on the season, and on vigilance in watching for and taking advantage of a lead. In 1872, Captain David Gray, of Peterhead, in the whaler ' Hope,' saw a wide extent of open water, with a water sky to the northward, on this east coast; and in 1874 he reported a great and unusual drift of the ice in the Spitzbergen sea.

90. On the whole, the East Greenland route ranks next to Smith Sound, as a promising direction to take with a view to exploring an important section of the unknown Polar area. It complies with all the conditions of success—navigation along a coast line, possibility of finding winter quarters beyond the threshold of the unknown region, and the means of exploring by sledge parties. A depôt ship would be established at or near the Pendulum Islands, while the advanced vessel would only have to reach about the 78th parallel in order to be within the unknown area, and so to make some measure of success certain. The recent investigation ought to ensure immunity from scurvy, and with a healthy crew the sledging operations over such ice as is described by the Germans, could be extended four degrees farther north at least, to the 82nd parallel. This would bring them within a short distance of Beaumont's farthest, and the discovery of Greenland would thus be completed—one of the most important geographical achievements that remains to be accomplished by this generation. The east coast is reported to be frequented by musk oxen, and its ice floes by bears and seals; so that the explorers would be able to obtain fresh provisions, while the winter darkness would be much shorter, and the climate less rigorous than that to which the late Expedition was exposed. The magnificent mountains and fjords of this east coast present features of peculiar interest in several branches of science, and it is probable that the various

discoveries made by explorers who will complete the circuit of Greenland will be of great value.

91. On the whole, then, the East Greenland route is the best that can be selected for a new Expedition; because it offers greater facilities and better chances of success, and also because by it the important discoveries of the Expedition of 1875–76 will best be followed up and made continuous. But there are at least four routes from which to select, namely, those of Jones Sound, East Greenland, and Franz Josef Land, and the North-east Passage. The reasons for continuing the work are as strong as those for commencing it; and I would earnestly submit that the Council of the Royal Geographical Society ought not to relax its efforts after one success, but that there should be continuity in its measures, and that, through good report and evil report, it should steadily persevere until the exploration of the unknown region round the North Pole is completed.

CLEMENTS R. MARKHAM.

LONDON: PRINTED BY WILLIAM CLOWES AND SONS, STAMFORD STREET AND CHARING CROSS.

THE

ARCTIC NAVY LIST.

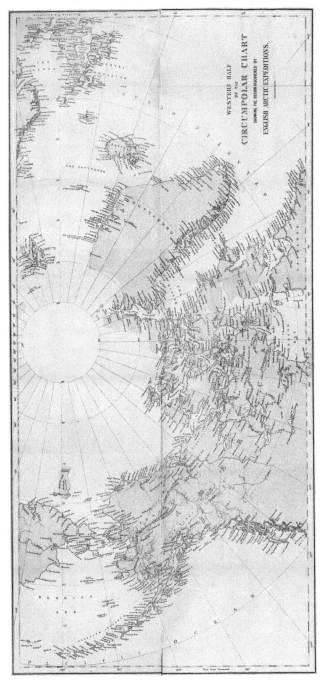

The material originally positioned here is too large for reproduction in this reissue. A PDF can be downloaded from the web address given on page iv of this book, by clicking on 'Resources Available'.

THE ARCTIC NAVY LIST;

OR,

A CENTURY

OF

ARCTIC & ANTARCTIC OFFICERS,

1773—1873.

TOGETHER WITH A LIST OF OFFICERS OF THE 1875 EXPEDITION,
AND THEIR SERVICES.

ATTEMPTED BY

CLEMENTS R. MARKHAM, C.B., F.R.S.

(AUTHOR OF "THE THRESHOLD OF THE UNKNOWN REGION.")

1875.

GRIFFIN & CO.,

(Publishers, by Appointment, to H.R.H. the Duke of Edinburgh,)

15, COCKSPUR STREET,   AND 2, THE HARD,
PALL MALL, LONDON.   PORTSEA, PORTSMOUTH.

Price Three Shillings and Sixpence.

PRINTED AT THE OFFICE OF THE PUBLISHERS.

PREFACE.

THE Arctic Navy List is an attempt to give a complete enumeration of all Officers who have served in the Arctic or Antarctic Regions in the Century between 1773 and 1873.* There have been Three Generations of Arctic Officers. First, that of COOK and PHIPPS. Second, that of ROSS, PARRY, FRANKLIN, and BACK. Third, that of the FRANKLIN searches. The fourth will commence with the Arctic Expedition of 1875.

Sir GEORGE BACK is the Father of Arctic Officers, and that illustrious explorer continues to take a warm interest in the labours and aspirations of his younger fellow workers in the glorious field of Polar research. JAMES ROSS, EDWARD BIRD, and HORATIO AUSTIN, who all served with PARRY, were also in the FRANKLIN searches. They formed the connecting link between the second and third generations of Arctic Officers. Thus the earlier experiences were handed down, and to CAPTAIN AUSTIN is due the praise of having organised those admirable arrangements for winter quarters which secured the bodily and mental health of officers and men when the spring travelling commenced. Sir LEOPOLD MCCLINTOCK, the disciple of Sir JAMES ROSS, far outstripped his master, and is the discoverer of naval sledge travelling. CAPTAIN NARES will be the connecting link between the third and fourth generations, and will hand down the traditions which represent the knowledge and experience acquired during the FRANKLIN searches.

The list gives the expedition or expeditions in which each Officer served. The most valuable qualifications for Arctic service are aptitude for taking part in those winter amusements which give life to the expedition during the months of forced inaction ; and for sledge travelling.* Under each officer is therefore given the part he took in the winter amusements, and the work he performed in the spring sledge travelling. Other services are given in many cases, and where any Officer is also an author, the titles of his work or works are quoted. Under the names of the different Officers, which have been commemorated on the Admiralty Charts, the Capes, Bays, Straits, Channels, or Islands, bearing those names are enumerated.†

The names of Officers who *wintered* in the Arctic Regions are in SMALL CAPITALS, and those of Officers who only made *summer* cruises are in *italics*.

The principal Civilian Arctic Navigators, such as PENNY, KENNEDY, SHEDDON, LAMONT, and LEIGH SMITH have been included in the list.

The List of Officers is followed by a List of Vessels in which they served in the Arctic Regions, also alphabetically arranged, so that an enquirer on seeing the ship in which any Officer served, can at once turn to the list of ships and see where the particular vessel wintered, and to what expedition she belonged.

The Circumpolar Chart, which is appended by permission of the Hydrographer, will be found useful for reference.†

---

* The names of Staff-Commander Aylen and Mr. Osborne, (boatswain,) have unfortunately been omitted in their proper places, but will be found as Addenda at the end of the list.

† The geographical names referred to in the List are not all on the Circumpolar Chart, owing to the small scale ; but they will all be found on the larger scale Admiralty Charts of the Arctic Sea, Nos. 2177, 2443, 2172, and also Discoveries in the Arctic Sea, No. 2118.

CONTENTS.

A CENTURY

OF

Arctic and Antarctic Officers,

1773—1873.

ABERNETHY, THOMAS.—In the *Hecla* (Parry), 1827, in the attempt to reach the Pole. Second Mate of the *Victory*, (J. Ross,) 1829-33. Gunner of the *Erebus*, (J. C. Ross,) 1839-43, in the Antarctic Expedition. Second Mate of the *Felix*, (J. Ross,) 1850-51. Chief Mate of the *Isabel*, (Inglefield,) 1852. He died at Peterhead on April 13th, 1860.

Cape Abernethy, on the north side of Wolstenholme Sound.

ADAMS, C.—Assistant-Surgeon of the *Enterprise*, (Collinson,) 1850-55. He was the companion of Lieutenant Barnard (whom see) when he was murdered.

ALDRICH, ROBERT DAWES.—Entered the Navy, January 22nd, 1824. Mate, 1830. Lieutenant, 1842. First Lieutenant of the *Resolute*, (Austin,) 1850-51. Gave Lectures to the men on Arctic Exploration during the winter. In the sledge travelling he was away, laying out a depôt on Somerville Island, from October 2nd to 5th, 1850. In the spring, starting April 15, he was away 62 days, went over 550 miles : average rate 9½ miles a day. 1860, retired Captain, F.R.G.S.

Cape Aldrich, on the west-coast of Bathurst Island.

ALLARD, J. H.—Second Master of the *Investigator*, (Bird,) 1848-49. Of the *Pioneer*, (Osborn,) 1850-51. Master of the *Pioneer*, (Osborn), 1852-54. Acted Charles in the "*Irish Tutor*," November, 1852. Staff-Commander, 1866.

Allard Island, off the north-coast of Bathurst Island.

ALLEN, ROBERT CALDER.—Master of the *Resolute*, (Austin,) 1850-51. Led a travelling party to search Lowther and Garrett Islands ; away 18 days and marched 137 miles. Retired Staff-Captain, 1870. F.R.G.S.

> *Allen Bay*, on the south-coast of Cornwallis Island.

Allen, G. H.—Master's Assistant in the *Herald*, (Kellett,) 1845-51. Second Master in the *President* (flag of Admiral Price) in the Pacific. Master of the *Trident* on the coast of Africa, and of the *Hornet*, (Dayman,) in the Red Sea as Assistant-Surveyor. Now a retired Staff-Commander, 1871.

ALLISON, J.—Greenland Master of the *Alexander*, (Parry,) 1818 ; of the *Hecla*, (Parry), 1819-20, and 1824-25.

> *Allison Bluff*, in Lyon Inlet.
> *Allison Bay*, in Melville Bay.

ALSTON, A. H.—Mate in the *North Star*, (Pullen,) 1852-53. Went home in the *Phœnix*, 1853. Since deceased.

ANDERSON, HENRY.—Mate of the *Prince Albert*, (Forsyth,) 1850-51, and of the same ship (Kennedy,) 1851-52.

Anderson, W.—Surgeon of the *Resolution*, (Cook,) 1776-79.

Anderson, R.—Gunner of the *Resolution*, (Cook,) 1776-79.

ANDERSON, R.—Surgeon of the *Investigator*, (Bird,) 1848-49 ; and of the *Enterprise*, (Collinson,) 1850-55.

> *Anderson Bay*, on Victoria Land, near Cambridge Bay.

Anderson, John Brett.—Midshipman in the *Herald*, (Kellett,) 1845-51.

ARMSTRONG, ALEXANDER,—Surgeon of the *Investigator*, (Mc'Clure,) 1850-54. 1866, Director General of the Medical Department, K.C.B., F.R.S., F.R.G.S., L.L.D. Author of "*Personal Narrative of the Discovery of the North-West Passage.*" 1857.

> *Armstrong Point* on the west-coast of Prince Albert Land.

AUSTIN, HORATIO THOMAS.—Entered the Navy in 1813. Served in the American War, in the *Ramillies* and *Creole* under Sir Thomas Hardy. Lieutenant, 1822. First Lieutenant of the *Fury*, (Hoppner,) 1824-25 ; and of the *Chanticleer* (Foster,) 1827-30. Commander, 1831. Commanded the first steamer in the service, the *Salamander*, 1832 ; *Medea*, 1834. Captain, 1838, of the *Cyclops*; 1839-43 in the Syrian War, and captured Sidon. C.B. *Blenheim*, 1848. Captain of H.M.S. *Resolute* 1850-51, and commanding the expedition. An admirable organizer of arrangements for winter quarters. Gave a grand *Bal Masqué* on January 12th, 1851. Captain Superintendent of Deptford Dockyard during the Crimean War. Admiral Superintendent of Malta Dockyard, 1863. K.C.B. Died 1865.

Austin Channel, between Byam Martin and Bathurst Isles.
Cape Austin on the west-coast of Cornwallis Isle.

BACK, GEORGE.—Born at Stockport in 1796. Entered the Navy in 1808 in the *Arethusa*, and served in boat actions on the north coast of Spain. Made prisoner when 14 were killed out of 18, and detained at Verdun until 1814. Served in the *Akbar* and *Bulwark*. Mate in the *Trent*, (Franklin,) 1818, in the Spitzbergen voyage. In Franklin's Land Expedition to the Copper-mine river and along the coast, 1819-22, surveyed and drew the charts. In Franklin's narrative we read : " Here we met Mr. Back, to whom, under Providence, we felt our lives were owing." Lieutenant, 1821. In the *Superb* in the West Indies and Lisbon, 1822-24. In Franklin's Second Land Expedition, 1825-27, and surveyed as far as Return Reef. Commander, 1827. Led an Expedition in search of Ross, in 1833-35; and discovered the Back River, tracing it for 500 miles to its mouth. Captain, 1835, by Order in Council. King William IV. said to him, " You and I, Sir, are the only two Captains by order in Council in the navy." Captain of the *Terror* in the voyage to Frozen Strait, 1836-37. Gold Medallist and F.R.G.S., 1835, and Gold Medal of the Paris G.S., F.R.S., D.C.L. Knighted, 1839. Author of " *Narrative of the Arctic Land Expedition to the mouth of the Great Fish River* " (1836), *and* " *Narrative of an Expedition in H.M.S. Terror* (1838.)" Most of the illustrations in the narratives of Franklin's Land Expeditions are from his sketches, as well as those in the narrative of the discovery of the Great Fish River.

Back, or Great Fish River.
Cape Back on the coast of Arctic America.
Point Back, up Smith Sound, so named by Dr. Kane.
Back Inlet on the coast of Zichy land (Austrian discoveries).

Bailey William.—Observer in the *Discovery*, (Clarke,) 1776-80, in Cook's Expedition.

BANCE, HENRY PRESCOTT.—Born at the Cape, 1831, son of Captain Bance, R.N. In the *Winchester*, (C. Eden,) 1844-46.

Midshipman in the *Assistance*, (Ommanney,) 1850-51. Lieutenant, 1852. Went to Australia 1855 ; Inspector of Post Offices at Melbourne. Retired Commander, 1867.

Bance Point in Ommanney Bay, Prince of Wales' Land.

Barden *Mr.*— Engineer of the *Isabel*, (Inglefield,) 1852.

Barlow, *J. C.*— Volunteer in the *Blossom*, (Beechey,) 1825. Retired Captain, 1865.

BARNARD, J. J.—Third Lieutenant of the *Investigator*, (Bird,) 1848-49. Led a travelling party from Port Leopold to the north shore of Barrow Strait. Second Lieutenant of the *Enterprise* (Collinson), 1850-51. Landed at Michaelowski, in the Russian-American territory to enquire into a rumour, and was brutally murdered by Kayukok Indians in a surprise of the Russian post of Darabin, near Norton Sound. See *Osborn's McClure's N.W. Passage, 4th edition, page 134.*

Barrett, *William.*—Purser of the *Trent*, (Franklin,) 1818.

BEECHEY, F. W.—Son of the artist, Sir W. Beechey. Born 1796, and entered the Navy in 1806. At the New Orleans action in the *Venguer*; Lieutenant of the *Trent*, (Franklin,) 1818 ; First Lieutenant of the *Hecla*, (Parry,) 1819-20. In winter quarters at Melville Island he was Manager of the " Royal Arctic Theatre." The plays acted were :—

" *The Mayor of Garratt ;*"	"*Bon Ton ;*"
" *The Citizen ;*"	"*The Liar ;*"
" *A bold stroke for a Wife ;*"	"*Miss in her Teens ;*"

and " *The N.W. Passage, or the Voyage Finished,*" an original musical entertainment. Beechey acted Miss Biddy in "*Miss in her Teens ;*" Philpot in " *The Citizen ;*" Jerry Sneak in " *The Mayor of Garratt ;*" Lady Minnikin in " *Bon Ton ;*" and Simon Pure in " *A bold stroke for a Wife.*"

Commander, 1822, of H.M.S. *Blossom ;* up Behring's Strait 1825-28 ; on a voyage intended to act in concert with Parry and Franklin. He extended the discovery of the American coast from Icy Cape (Cook's furthest) to Point Barrow. Captain, 1827. Retired Admiral, F.R.S. ; President, R.G.S. (and original member), 1856, in which year he died. *Obituary notice, R.G.S.J., vol. xxvi. p. xcv.*

Author of " *Narrative of a voyage to Behring's Strait to co-operate with the Polar Expeditions in H.M.S. ' Blossom.'* " (1831)

" *Voyage of discovery towards the North Pole, performed in H.M.S. ' Dorothea' and ' Trent,' in 1818."* (1843.)

" *Proceedings of the Expedition, to explore the north coast of Africa from Tripoli eastward."* (1828.)

Beechey Island, off the S.W. end of North Devon.

Cape Beechey, on the north shore of Liddon's Gulf.

Beechey Point, on the American Coast near Point Barrow.

Beechey, R. B.—Midshipman in the *Blossom,* (Beechey,) 1825-29. Retired Captain, 1857.

BEEMAN, ROBERT.—Boatswain of the *Erebus,* (J. C. Ross,) 1839-43, in the Antarctic Expedition. 1845, Foreman of Riggers at Woolwich. 1845, Master Rigger at Chatham. 1851, Boatswain of Chatham yard. 1865, Chief Boatswain. Retired, 1870.

BELCHER, EDWARD.—Born in 1799, and entered the Navy in 1812. Assistant Surveyor in the *Blossom,* (Beechey,) 1825-28. Commander, 1829. Surveying in the *Ætna* on the West Coast of Africa, from 1832 to 1834. Commander of the *Sulphur* in the voyage round the world, 1836-42. Captain, 1841. C.B. for the taking of the Bogue Forts. Knighted, 1843. In command of the surveying ship *Samarang,* 1842-47, in the Eastern Archipelago. Captain of the *Assistance,* and in command of the Arctic Expedition, 1852-54. Abandoned his ship and tender *(Pioneer)* in Wellington Channel, and ordered the *Resolute* and *Intrepid* to be abandoned, 1854. F.R.G.S. *(original member),* K.C.B. Retired Admiral.

> Author of " *A Treatise on Nautical Surveying."* (1834.)
>
> " *Narrative of a Voyage Round the World in H.M.S. ' Sulphur.' "* (1843.)
>
> " *Narrative of the Voyage of H.M.S. ' Samarang.' "* (1848.)
>
> " *The last of the Arctic Voyages."* (1855. 2 vols.)
>
> *Belcher Point,* on the north coast of North Devon.
>
> *Belcher Channel,* between Grinnell Land and North Cornwall.

BELL, T.—Assistant-Surgeon in the *Fury,* (Hoppner,) 1804-25.

BELLOT, JOSEPH RENE.—Lieutenant in the French Navy. Officer of the Legion of Honor. Served in the *Prince Albert,* (Kennedy,) 1851-52 ; in the *Phœnix,* (Inglefield,) 1853.

Drowned in Wellington Channel on his way from Beechey Island to the *Assistance*, on August 18th, 1853. Monument in front of Greenwich Hospital. (See *Obituary Notice, R.G.S.J.*, vol. *xxiv.*, *p. lxxvi.*)

Author of "*Journal d'un Voyage aux Mers Polaires.*" (Paris, 1854.)

Bellot Strait, separating the extreme north point of America from North Somerset.

Bellot Point, on the east coast of Wellington Channel.

BEVERLEY, J. C.—Assistant-Surgeon in the *Isabella*, (J. Ross,) 1818, and in the *Griper*, (Liddon,) 1819-20. Surgeon in the *Hecla*, (Parry,) 1827; and in the boat with Parry in the attempt to reach the Pole. In the winter, at Melville Island, he was in the company of the "*Royal Arctic Theatre*," and acted the Aunt in "*Miss in her Teens*"; Lint, in the "*Mayor of Garratt*"; and Simon Pure in "*A Bold stroke for a Wife.*" In 1828 he left the service, and went into private practice. In 1857 he applied to be reinstated, but the Admiralty refused. He died soon afterwards.

Crimson Cliffs of Beverley, near Cape York (Greenland).
Beverley Inlet, on the south coast of Melville Island.
Beverley Bay, on the north coast of Spitzbergen.

BIGGS, JAMES.—Purser of the *Enterprise*, (J. C. Ross,) 1848-49.
Point Biggs, on the east coast of Prince of Wales' Land.

Billings, W. J.—Assistant-Surgeon in the *Herald*, (Kellett,) 1845-50. He served through the Russian War. Now retired.

BIRD, EDWARD.—Entered the Navy in 1812. At the battle of Algiers, 1816. Midshipman in the *Hecla*, (Lyon,) 1821-23; in the *Fury*, (Hoppner,) 1824-25. In the *Hecla*, (Parry,) 1827, serving in the boat with J. C. Ross, in the attempt to reach the Pole. *The only surviving British officer (out of four) who has been in 82° 45′ N.* First Lieutenant of the *Medea*, (Austin,) 1834. First Lieutenant of the *Erebus*, (J. C. Ross,) in the Antarctic Expedition, 1839-43. Commander, 1841. Captain, 1843. Captain of the *Investigator*, 1848-49. Retired Vice Admiral, 1869.

Cape Bird, the south west point of North Somerset.
Bird Island, in Hoppner Strait.
Bird Bay, on the north coast of Spitzbergen.

BISCOE, JOHN.—Master, R.N. Made a voyage to the Antarctic Ocean in the brig *Tula*, belonging to Messrs. Enderby, in 1830-32. In 1831 he discovered land in 67° S., which was named " Enderby Land" ; and other islands named " Graham Land." *Gold Medallist, R.G.S.* See *R.G.S.J. iii., p. 105.*

Bisson, P.—Midshipman of the *Alexander*, (Parry,) 1818.
Cape Bisson on the coast of Greenland.

BLANKY, T.—First mate of the *Victory*, (Ross,) 1829-33. Ice Master of the *Terror*, (Crozier,) 1845-48.

Bligh, William.—Master of the *Resolution*, (Cook,) 1776-79. Afterwards Captain of the *Bounty*.

BODIE, JAMES.—Master of the *Pagoda*, (Moore,) in the Antarctic Expedition of 1845. Now a retired Staff-Captain.

Borland, W. G.—Assistant Surgeon of *Dorothea*, (Buchan,) 1818.

BOUCHIER, THOMAS.—Second Master of the *Plover*, (Moore,) 1848-50. Master of the *Rattlesnake*, (Trollope,) 1853. He was afterwards Senior Assistant to Captain Cox in the Victoria Survey, and died at Melbourne in 1866.

BRADFORD, ABRAHAM ROSE.—Surgeon of the *Resolute*, (Austin,) 1850-51. Led an extended sledge party to the east coast of Melville Island, away 80 days, and went over 669 miles. Now a retired Deputy Inspector of Hospitals.
Bradford Point, N.E. point of Melville Island.

BRANDS, GEORGE.—Engineer in the *Fox*, (McClintock,) 1857-58. He died of apoplexy, in winter quarters, on November 6th, 1858.

BROMLEY, JOHN.—Carpenter of the *Erebus*, (J. C. Ross,) 1839-43, in the Arctic Expedition. He died in 1873.

BROOMAN, JOHN E.—Purser of the *Resolute*, (Austin,) 1850-51. In the Company of the " *Royal Arctic Theatre ;*" acted Mr. Wiffles in " *Done on both sides ;*" and King Artaxominous in " *Bombastes Furioso.*" He died suddenly at Hull, in September, 1858.
Point Brooman on the east coast of McDougall Bay.

Brothers, J. E.—Gunner in the *Hecla*, (Parry,) 1824-25.

BROWNE, W. H. J.—Son of the harbour master at Dublin. Originally in the merchant service; joined the *Sulphur*, (Belcher,) at the Fiji Islands, as Master's Assistant. In the *Samarang*, (Belcher,) when he became a Mate. Second Lieutenant of the *Enterprise,* (J. C. Ross,) 1848-49. Led a sledge party from Port Leopold to the east coast of Prince Regent's Inlet. Second Lieutenant of the *Resolute,* (Austin,) 1850-51. Scene painter to the "*Royal Arctic Theatre.*" In the sledge travelling went over 375 miles in 43 days, down Peel Sound. An admirable artist. His sketches of Arctic scenery at Port Leopold were published by Ackermann, 1849. He also assisted in painting the Arctic Panorama in Leicester Square. Retired Commander, 1864. He died at Woolwich in 1872.

Browne Bay, on the east coast of Prince of Wales' land.

Bruce, P.—Greenland Master of the *Dorothea,* (Buchan,) 1818.

BRUNTON, J.—Midshipman of the *Hecla,* (Parry,) 1824-25. Many years a Lieutenant in the Coast-guard.

BRUNTON, A.—First Engineer of the *Victory,* (Ross,) 1829-33.

Buchan, David.—Several years serving on the coast of Newfoundland, and made a journey across the interior. Commander, 1816. Captain of the *Dorothea* in the Spitzbergen voyage, 1818. Returned to Newfoundland as Captain of the *Grasshopper,* 1820-23. Gave Franklin much assistance in fitting out his land expeditions. Lost on his passage home in the *Upton Castle,* Indiaman, in 1838.

Buchan Bay, on the coast of Arctic America.

BURDON, WILLIAM.—Midshipman in the *Pagoda,* (Moore,) in the Antarctic Expedition of 1845. Since deceased.

Burney, James.—Son of Dr. Burney, the great Greek scholar, and grandson of Charles Burney, author of the "*History of Music.*" Born 1759, and served in Cook's second voyage. First Lieutenant of the *Discovery,* (Cook,) 1776-80 ; up Behring's Strait, in Cook's third expedition. Rear-Admiral ; and an eminent geographer. Died 1821.

Author of a "*Chronological History of the Discoveries in the South Sea or Pacific Ocean, by James Burney, Captain, Royal Navy.*" (4to, 5 vols. 1803.)

Also of a History of Russian discoveries on the coast of Siberia.

BUSHNAN, JOHN.—Clerk in the *Isabella,* (Ross,) 1818. Midshipman in the *Hecla,* (Parry,) 1819-20. In the company of the "*Royal Arctic Theatre.*" He acted Captain Flash in "*Miss in her Teens*"; Quilldrive in the "*Citizen*"; Major Sturgeon in the "*Mayor of Garratt*"; Landlord in the "*N. W. Passage*";

Mignon in "*Bon Ton*"; and Sackbut in a "*Bold stroke for a Wife.*" Assistant-Surveyor of the *Fury*, (Parry,) 1821-23. He was appointed to Franklin's Expedition, but died before starting in 1825.

> *Bushnan Cove*, at the further end of Liddon's Gulf.

> *Bushnan Island*, in Frozen Strait.

> *Bushnan Island*, near Cape York, in Melville Bay (Greenland).

Castell, William.—Clerk in charge of the *Trent*, (Franklin), 1818.

CATOR, JOHN BERTIE.—Was mate in the *Wellesley*, and in the *Herald*, (Joe Nias,) in the China War. Lieutenant, 1842; in the *Virago* 1843-46 in the Mediterranean. Lieutenant commanding the *Intrepid* in the Arctic Expedition of 1850-51. Manager of the "*Royal Intrepid Saloon.*" Acted General Ducker in "*Charles XII.*" Retired Captain, 1867. Conservator of the Humber.

> *Cator Harbour*, in Sherard Osborn Isle, off the north coast of Bathurst Island.

CHAMPION, GEORGE.—Greenland Mate of the *Hecla*, (Parry,) 1824-25.

Charlton, John F.—Surgeon of the *Phænix*, (Inglefield,) 1853. Since deceased

Chermside, Lieut., R.E.—Accompanied Mr. Leigh Smith in his voyage to Spitzbergen in 1873, and took numerous photographs.

CHEYNE, JOHN P.—Son of Captain Cheyne, R.N., an old friend of Sir Edward Parry. Master's Assistant in the surveying ship *Columbia*, in the Bay of Fundy. Midshipman in the *Enterprise*, (J. C. Ross,) 1848-49. Mate in the *Resolute*, (Austin,) 1850-51. Acted Distaffina in "*Bombastes Furioso.*" Led an auxiliary sledge party in the Melville Island division, when he was 12 days away, and marched 126 miles. Lieutenant in the *Assistance*, (Belcher,) 1852-54. Acted Rosa in the "*Irish Tutor*," and Marianne in the "*Silent Woman.*" Led an auxiliary sledge party. Retired Commander, 1870.

> Author of a "*History of the Arctic Expedition of 1848-49*," published in numbers.

> *Cheyne Islands*, off the north-east coast of Bathurst Island.

> *Cheyne Point*, at the east end of Griffith Island.

Chimmo, William.—A Mate of the *Herald*, (Kellett,) 1845-51. Commanded the *Torch*, tender to the *Herald*, in the survey of the south-west Pacific. Since commanded the *Gannet*, surveying in the West Indies; and the *Nassau* in the Eastern Archipelago. Now retired.

Clavering, D. C.—Commander of the *Pheasant*, 1820-22, with Captain Sabine, conducting pendulum observations in the Atlantic. Commander of the *Griper*, in the voyage with Captain Sabine, to Spitzbergen and the east coast of Greenland, 1823. Commander of the *Redwing* on the coast of Africa, 1827, and lost in her.

Clarke, Charles.—Captain of the *Discovery*, 1776-79, in Cook's Expedition to Behring's Strait. He commanded the expedition from the date of Cook's death to his own. He died on board the *Discovery*, on August 22nd, 1779. He had been second Lieutenant of the *Resolution* in Cook's second voyage.

CLERK, HENRY.—Lieutenant R.A., in the *Pagoda*, (Moore,) in the Antarctic Expedition of 1845, in charge of magnetic observations. Now Major-General, R.A., F.R.S.

Cleverley, John.—Lieutenant in the *Racehorse*, (Phipps,) 1773. Several of the illustrations in Lord Mulgrave's work are from his sketches.

Cleverly, James.—Carpenter of the *Resolution*, (Cook,) 1776-80.

Collie, A.—Surgeon of the *Blossom*, (Beechey,) 1825-28.

COLLINS, H. F.—Second Master of the *Erebus*, (Franklin,) 1845-48.
  " The very essence of good nature and good humour."—*(Fitzjames.)*

COLLINSON, RICHARD.—Entered the Navy in 1823. Midshipman in the *Chanticleer*, (Foster,) 1829-31. In the *Ætna* on the West Coast of Africa with Belcher in 1832. Served in the *Sulphur*, (Belcher,) 1835 to 1838, and in the *Wellesley* during the first China war, and at the storming of Chusan. Commander, 1841. Commander of the *Plover*, 1842-46, piloting during the operations up the Yang-tsze. Captain, 1842, and C.B. for his distinguished services in China. Captain of the *Enterprise* in the Arctic Expedition of 1850-55. In the sledge travelling of 1852 he left the ship in winter quarters in Prince Albert Sound on April 14th. Explored the east coast of Prince of Wales Strait as far as Collinson Inlet, and returned on June 16th, away 51 days. In the travelling of 1853 he was absent 49 days, marching from Cambridge Bay, in Dease Strait, to Gateshead Island. F.R.G.S. (Gold medallist 1858.) Elder Brother of the Trinity House. Retired Vice-Admiral.

It is universally regretted among geographers, that Admiral Collinson has never published his narrative of his very important Arctic voyage.

Editor of "*The Three Voyages of Martin Frobisher in search of a passage to Cathaia by the north west*" (for the Hakluyt Society, 1867).

Cape Collinson, on Victoria Land, near his furthest.

Cape Collinson, on the S.E. coast of Banks' Island.

Collinson Inlet, on the north shore of Prince Albert Land.

Collinson Inlet, on the north-west shore of King William's Land.

Collinson Fiord, on the coast of Zichy Land (Austrian discoveries).

Collinson, T. B.—Nephew of the above. Midshipman in the *Herald*, (Kellett,) 1845-51. Lieutenant in the *Royalist*, (Bate,) surveying the China Seas ; and afterwards commanded the *Spy* on the coast of Brazil.

Colomb, Philip.—In the *Phœnix*, (Inglefield,) 1854. Captain, 1870. Inventor of a system of night signals, and of a lamp for lighting lower decks. Commanded the *Dryad* on the east coast of Africa. Author of "*Slave catching in the Indian Ocean*" (1873). Captain, 1870. Flag Captain of the *Audacious* on the China Station, 1874.

Cook, James.—Born at Marton, in Yorkshire, on October 27th, 1728. Joined the *Eagle* as A.B. 1775. Master of the *Mercury*, 1759. Surveyor in Newfoundland, 1763. He commanded the *Endeavour* in his first voyage of discovery as Lieutenant, 1768. Observed the transit of Venus at Tahiti, 1769. Second voyage, 1772-75. Captain of the *Resolution*, 1776-79, and commanding the expedition to discover the N.W. Passage by way of Behring Strait. Passed Behring Strait, and discovered the coast of Arctic America as far as Icy Cape, and Arctic Asia between Cape North and Cape Serdze. Murdered at Hawaii in February, 1779. F.R.S.

Author of the first two volumes of "*A voyage to the Pacific Ocean for making discoveries in the Northern Hemisphere*" (1784).

Cooper, E. J. L.—Entered the navy in 1827. Lieutenant in the *Herald*, (Kellett,) 1845-49, and *Plover*, (Moore,) 1849-51. He died at Southampton in 1852.

COTTER, P. P.—Master of the *Terror*, (Crozier,) in the Antarctic Expedition, 1839-43. Since deceased.

COUCH, EDWARD.—Mate in the *Erebus*, (Franklin,) 1845-48.
"A little black-haired, smooth-faced fellow, good humoured in his own way, writes, works, draws, all quietly."—*(Fitzjames.)*
Couch Pass, between Baillie Hamilton and Dundas Islands in Queen's Channel.

COURT, STEPHEN.—Born at Folkestone, on November 23rd, 1826. and educated at Greenwich Naval School. Served in the mail packet service between Folkestone and the Brazils. Second Master of the *Enterprise*, (J. C. Ross,) 1848-49; and master of the *Investigator*, (M'Clure,) 1850-54. Accompanied M'Clure in the sledge journey from October 21st to 31st in 1850, when the N.W. Passage was discovered, and of the greatest assistance to him throughout this trying commission. Made several sledge journeys in 1854, in connection with Sir E. Belcher's abandonment of the ships, and consequent retreat of the crews. In the *Odin*, (Wilcox), during the Crimean war, and at the bombardment of Kinburn. Master of the *Furious*, (Sherard Osborn,) in China and Japan, 1857-59. Harbour-Master of Shanghae, 1859-61. He died at Folkestone on April 11th, 1861.
Court Point, on Banks Island.

COWIE, ROBERT.—Surgeon of the *Prince Albert*, (Kennedy,) 1851-52.

Crane, Mr.—Master of the *Racehorse*, (Phipps,) 1773, in the Spitzbergen voyage.

CRAWFORD, GEORGE.—Greenland Mate in the *Dorothea*, (Buchan,) 1818; in the *Hecla*, (Parry,) 1819-20; and in the *Fury*, (Parry,) 1821-23.
Crawford Island, off the east point of Winter Island.

Crawley, John.—A volunteer in the *Blossom*, (Beechey,) 1825-28.

CRESSWELL, SAMUEL G.—Mate in the *Investigator*, (Bird,) 1848-49. Second Lieutenant in the *Investigator*, (McClure,) 1850-54. In the sledge travelling of 1851 he left the ship on April 18th and returned May 20th, having been absent 32 days, and explored 170 miles of Banks Island. Returned home in the *Phœnix*, 1853. Since deceased. He was a good artist, and his water-color sketches of scenes in the voyage of the *Investigator* were lithographed.

CROZIER, FRANCIS RAWDEN MOIRA.—Born at Bowbridge in co. Down, in 1800. Entered the Navy in 1810. Midshipman in the *Fury*, (Parry,) 1821-23. In the company of the "*Royal Arctic Theatre*," and acted Sir Lucius O'Trigger in "*The Rivals*." In the *Hecla*, (Parry,) 1827, in the Spitzbergen voyage. First Lieutenant of the *Cove*, (J. C. Ross,) 1836. Captain of the *Terror* in the Antarctic Expedition, 1839-43. Captain, 1841. Captain of the *Terror*, 1845-48. Landed on King Williams' Land in command of the retreating crews, abandoning the ships on April 22nd, 1848.

Crozier Channel, between Eglington and Prince Patrick Islands.

Cape Crozier, the west point of King William Land.

Cape Crozier, west entrance of the Bay of Mercy, Banks Island.

Crozier River, falling into Hooper Inlet, near Fury and Hecla Strait.

Crozier Bay, on the west coast of Prince of Wales' Land.

Point Crozier, in Treurenbury Bay, Spitzbergen.

Crozier Strait, between Bathurst and Cornwallis Isles.

Cumming, Mr.—Lieutenant in the *Racehorse*, (Phipps,) 1773. Took the pendulum observations.

DAVIS, JOHN E.—Second Master in the *Terror*, (Crozier) 1839-43, in the Antarctic Expedition. Surveyor to the North Atlantic Telegraph Expedition in the *Fox*, 1862. Now Naval Assistant to the Hydrographer. Retired Staff-Captain, 1870. Author (jointly with his son) of the *Azimuth Tables*. Inventor of an improved sextant. He drew the charts for the Antarctic Expedition ; and the illustrations in the "*Narrative of Sir James Ross*," are from his drawings. F.R.G.S.

Dauvergne, P.—Lieutenant of the *Racehorse*, (Phipps,) 1773. The illustrations in Lord Mulgrave's work are partly from his sketches.

DEALY, WILLIAM JUSTIN.—First entered as A.B. in the *Ramillies* in 1807. Served through the American war. Mate in the *Dorothea*, (Buchan,) 1818. In the *Hecla*, (Parry,) 1819-20. Lieutenant, 1820, but did not serve again.

Dealy Island, on the south coast of Melville Island.

DEAN, WILLIAM.—Carpenter in the *Investigator*, (Bird,) 1848-49 ; in the *Assistance* (Ommanney,) 1850-51 ; and in the *Resolute*, (Kellett,) 1852-54. He had the entire control of the scenic arrangements of the *Royal Arctic Theatre*, in 1850-51 and 1852-54 ; and of the carpentering work in the sledge equipments.　Carpenter of the *Marlborough*, 1858-61.　In the Transport Department 1863 to 1873.　Retired, September, 1873.

Dean Point, in Ommanney Bay, Prince of Wales' Land.

De BRAY, EMILE.—Enseigne de Vaisseau in the French Navy.　In the *Resolute*, (Kellett,) 1852-54.　In the autumn travelling of 1852, he was away 17 days, and went over 175 miles.　In the spring sledge travelling of 1853, he was auxiliary to Mc'Clintock, 45 days absent, and travelled 440 miles : rate, 8 miles a day.

Cape De Bray, on the west coast of Melville Island.

DES VŒUX, C. F.—In the *Cornwallis* and *Endymion*.　Mate in the *Erebus*, (Franklin,) 1845-48.

"A most unexceptionable, clever, agreeable, light-hearted, obliging, young fellow."—*(Fitzjames.)*

He was in a travelling party with Graham Gore to King William's Land, in May, 1847.

Des Vœux Island, in Queen's Channel.

DICKSON, WALTER.—Assistant-Surgeon in the *Winchester*, flag-ship at the Cape, 1843-45.　In medical charge of the *Pagoda* in the Antarctic Expedition of 1845.　Two years in the Baltic during the Russian war.　Surgeon of H.M.S. *Cheasapeake*, in India and China, 1857-61.　Staff-Surgeon, 1859.　Retired, 1862.　Now Medical Inspector of H.M. Customs.　Author of "*Narrative of the Voyage of the Pagoda*," published in the "United Service Magazine" for May, June, July, 1850.

DOMVILLE, WILLIAM J., M.D.—Surgeon of the *Resolute*, (Kellett,) 1852-54.　On the committee of management of the *Royal Arctic Theatre*.　Acted Rochester in "*Charles II.*"　In the second winter he gave lectures on chemistry to the men.　In the spring sledge travelling in 1853 he was away 41 days, going over 323 miles, at a daily rate of 8 miles on one occasion, and 35 days on another; altogether, 76½ days, covering 640 miles.　Now a Deputy Inspector of Hospitals.

DONALDSON, J.—Gunner in the *Terror*, (Back,) 1836-37.　Died in February, 1837.

DONNET, JAMES J. L., M.D.—Surgeon in the *Assistance*,(Ommanney,) 1850-51.　Editor of the "*Aurora Borealis*," an Arctic newspaper.　Acted Mrs. Jewel in "*Did you ever send your Wife to Camberwell*."　Now Deputy-Inspector of Hospitals at Malta.

DONOVAN, J.—Surgeon of the *Terror*, (Back,) 1836-37.　Retired, 1861.　Now a retired Staff-Surgeon.

Duke, J.—Surgeon of the *Dorothea,* (Buchan,) 1818,

EDE, CHARLES.—Assistant-Surgeon in the *Assistance,* (Ommanney,) 1850-51.   Statuary and Sculptor to the expedition.   Author of a pantomime entitled, " *Zero, or, Harlequin Light,*" acted in the Arctic Regions, and of several Arctic songs.   Acted Mr. Crank in " *Did you ever send your Wife to Camberwell,*" Mrs. Wiffles in " *Done on both sides,*" and Adam Brock, in " *Charles XII.*"   Led an auxiliary sledge party to Cape Walker, 20 days away, and went over 175 miles.   Retired from the service in 1852.   Now in private practice residing near Guildford.

Edgar, I.—Master of the *Discovery,* (Clarke,) 1776-80, in Cook's expedition.

EDWARDS, J.—Surgeon of the *Isabella,* (Ross,) 1818; of the *Hecla,* (Parry,) 1819-20; of the *Fury,* (Parry,) 1821-23.   Acted Faulkland in the *Rivals* in 1822.

> *Cape Edwards* at east entrance of Lyon Inlet (Melville Peninsula.)

ELDER, ALEXANDER.—Greenland Mate in the *Griper,* (Liddon,) 1819-20, and in the *Hecla,* (Lyon,) 1821-23.   Died of dropsy 17th April, 1823.

ELLIOTT, JAMES.—Native of Landulph, in Cornwall.   Master of the *Agincourt* in the China war, and took her up the Yang-tsze. Second Lieutenant (to navigate) in the *Assistance,* (Ommanney,) 1850-51.   In the *Phœnix,* (Inglefield,) 1853, and 1854. Commander 1855, in the Coast Guard.   Died 1865.

ELLIOTT, W.—Clerk in charge of the *North Star,* (Pullen,) 1852-54. Paymaster of the *Plumper,* (Richards,) in the survey of Vancouver Island.

Elson, J.—Master of the *Blossom,* (Beechey,) 1825-28, in charge of the boat expedition that discovered Point Barrow.

Evans, Thomas.—Purser of the *Griper,* (Lyon,) 1824.

Evans, J.—Clerk in the *Blossom,* (Beachey,) 1825-28.

Ewin, William.—Boatswain of the *Resolute,* (Cook,) 1776-79.

FAIRHOLME, J. W.--Born in 1821.   Entered the navy in 1834.   In 1838, being in command of a prize, he was wrecked, captured by Moors in Senegal, and rescued by French negroes.   In 1839 he served on the coast of Syria.   In 1840 he joined

Captain Trotter's Niger Expedition, and ascended the river 350 miles, to Egga. Lieutenant, 1843. Joined the *Excellent* in 1843. Second Lieutenant in the *Erebus*, (Franklin,) 1845-48.

> " A most agreeable companion, and a well-informed man."—(*Fitzjames.*)

Fairholme Island off the west coast of Grinnell Land.

Fairholme Island off the west coast of King William's Land.

FAWCKNER, WILLIAM H.—At Greenwich school. Entered the navy as Master's Assistant in *H.M.S. Collingwood*, 1844-48. 2nd Master in the *Breadalbane*, transport, crushed by the ice off Beechey Island, 1853. Master, 1856. Now Staff-Commander of *Lord Warden*, Mediterranean Flag-ship, since 1874.

FIDDIS, J.—Carpenter of the *Hecla*, (Parry,) 1824-25.

FIFE, GEORGE.—Greenland Master of the *Trent*, (Franklin,) 1818, of the *Griper*, (Liddon,) 1819-20, and of the *Hecla*, (Lyon,) 1821-23. He died on August 6th, 1823.

FISHER, ALEXANDER.—Assistant-Surgeon of the *Alexander*, (Parry,) 1818, and of the *Hecla*, (Parry,) 1819-20. He accompanied Parry in the journey across Melville Island. Surgeon of the *Hecla*, (Lyon,) 1821-23.

Author of " *A Journal of a Voyage of Discovery to the Arctic Regions in H.M.S. ' Hecla,' 1819-20.*" (1821.)

Cape Fisher, on the west shore of Hecla and Griper Bay.

FISHER, REV. G., M.A.—Astronomer in the *Dorothea*, (Bucan,) 1818. Chaplain, 1821. Chaplain and astronomer in the *Fury*, (Parry,) 1821-23. In the *Spartiate* at Lisbon in 1827. In the *Victory*, 1832. Head Master of Greenwich School from 1834 to 1863. He died on May 14th, 1873.

Cape Fisher, the south west end of Winter Island.

FISHER, PETER.—Joined the navy in 1827. Mate in the *Terror*, (Back,) 1836-37. In the *Herald*, (Joe Nias,) in China, 1838. Lieutenant, 1838. Commander, 1841. Inspecting Commander of Coast Guard, 1841-48. Captain, 1848. He died in 1861.

Cape Fisher, on Southampton Island.

FITZJAMES, JAMES.—Entered the Navy in 1825. From 1834 to 1837 he served in the Euphrates Expedition. Lieutenant, 1838, in the *Excellent*. Served in the *Cornwallis*, 1840-42, in the China War. Commander, 1842, of the *Clio*, 1842-44. Settled disputes at Ichaboe, the guano deposit near the Cape.

Commander of the *Erebus*, (Franklin,) 1845-47 ; especially charged with the magnetic observations. Captain, 1847-48. Landed on King William's Land ; second in command of the retreating parties, abandoning the ships on April 22nd, 1848. F.R.G.S.

The last journals of Captain Fitzjames, sent home from · Greenland in 1845, were edited by W. Coningham, Esq., M.P., and privately printed at Brighton.

(See *Obituary Notice, R.G.S.J., xxv., p. lxxxvi.*)

Fitzjames Island and *Point*, in Queen's Channel.

Fitzjames Island, on the south coast of King William's Island.

FORD, G. F.—Carpenter of the *Investigator*, (M'Clure,) 1850-54.

Forsyth, Charles C.—Commander (R.N.) of the *Prince Albert*, Lady Franklin's searching schooner, 1850. Went down Prince Regent's Inlet, and returned the same year. He died a Captain, R.N.

FOSTER, HENRY.—Midshipman in the *Conway*, (Basil Hall,) in South America. First Lieutenant of the *Griper*, (Clavering,) 1823, in the .Spitzbergen voyage. Third Lieutenant of the *Hecla*, (Parry,) 1824-25 ; and took the magnetic observations. Second Lieutenant of the *Hecla*, (Parry,) 1827, and explored Hinlopen Strait, in Spitzbergen. His magnetic work was published in the Philosophical Transactions for 1826, for which he received the *Copley Medal*, F.R.S. Commander, 1827 ; his promotion and a ship being given him by the Duke of Clarence, Lord High Admiral, owing to his having obtained the *Copley Medal*. Commander of the *Chanticleer*, discovery ship, 1827-29. Drowned in the Chagres river, when engaged in determining the meridian distance between Chagres and Panama, 1829.

Foster Island.—In Hinlopen Strait, Spitzbergen.

FRANKLIN, JOHN.—Born in 1786, at Spilsby, in Lincolnshire. Entered the Navy in 1800. At the battle of Copenhagen in 1801. In 1803 served in the *Investigator*, under Captain Flinders, in the Australian Expedition ; and in 1804 he was Signal Officer in the famous action when Linois was defeated by Captain Dance. He served in the battle of Trafalgar as Signal Midshipman on board the *Bellerophon*. Wounded in the action at New Orleans. Lieutenant commanding the *Trent*, 1818, in the attempt to reach the Pole. In 1819 he commanded the land expedition down the Copper-mine river, returning in 1822. Commander, 1st January, 1821.

C

Captain, 1st January, 1822.   In 1823 he married Miss Eleanor Purdon, authoress of "*The Veils,*" "*The Arctic Expedition,*" and other poems.   She died in 1825, a few days after he sailed on his second expedition, leaving one daughter.   In 1825-27 he commanded the second land expedition to the shores of the Polar Sea.   In 1828 he married Jane, daughter of John Griffin, Esq.   *Knighted,* 1829, K.C.H., F.R.S., D.C.L., F.R.G.S., (*Original Member.*) 1830-34 he commanded the *Rainbow* in the Mediterranean. Made a Knight of the Order of Redeemer of Greece. Governor of Van Diemen's Land, 1838-44.   Captain of the *Erebus,* commanding the Arctic Expedition, 1845.   Rear-Admiral, 1847.   He died on June 11th, 1847, on board the *Erebus,* while beset to the north of King William's Island.

Author of "*The Narrative of a Journey to the shores of the Polar Sea in* 1819-20-21 *and* 22." (Murray, 1823.)

"*Narrative of a Second Expedition to the shores of the Polar Sea,*" 1825-26-27.   (Murray, 1828.)

See *Obituary Notice R.G.S.J., vol. xxv., p. lxxxvi.*   See also "*The career, last voyage, and fate of Sir John Franklin,*" by Sherard Osborn, (1860); and "*Notice Biographique de Sir John Franklin, par M. de la Roquette.*"

Lady Franklin, the noble-minded widow of the great discoverer, devoted many years to furthering the search for her lost husband and his comrades.   She fitted out and despatched the *Prince Albert* in 1850, and again in 1851, and the *Isabel* in 1852, and despatched the *Fox* in 1857; thus, through Sir L. McClintock, finally solving the question.   The R.G.S. Gold Medal was presented to Lady Franklin in 1860, in commemoration of Sir John's discoveries.

Franklin Point, on the N.W. coast of King William's Island.
Franklin Strait, south of Peel Sound.
Franklin Point, on the coast of America, near Icy Cape.
Franklin Point, east of the mouth of the Mackenzie river.

GAWLER, H. B.—Second Master in the *North Star,* (Saunders,) 1849-50.   Now a retired Navigating Lieutenant.

GERMAIN, B.—Purser of the *Dorothea,* (Buchan,) 1818; and of the *Hecla,* (Lyon,) 1821-23.

Gilfillan, A.—Assistant Surgeon of the *Trent,* (Franklin,) 1818.

GILPIN, J. D.—Clerk in charge of the *Investigator,* (Bird,) 1848-49.

Goodridge, J. O.—Surgeon in the *Herald*, (Kellett,) 1845-50. He died in 1865.

GOODSIR, HARRY.—Previously Curator of the Edinburgh Museum. An eminent naturalist. Author, with his brother, Professor Goodsir, F.R.S., of "*Anatomical and Pathological Observations,*" and of many other papers. Assistant Surgeon of the *Erebus,* (Franklin,) 1845-48.

"Perfectly good humoured, very well informed on general points, in natural history learned, and is a pleasant companion."—*Fitzjames.*

GOODSIR, R. ANSTRUTHER.—Brother of the above. Went a voyage in a whaler with Captain Penny, 1849. Surgeon of the *Lady Franklin,* (Penny,) in search of his brother. Explored the east and part of the north coast of Cornwallis Island by sledge in the spring of 1851.

Author of "*Arctic Voyage to Baffin's Bay in search of friends with Sir John Franklin,*" *1850.*

Goodsir Inlet, on the east coast of Bathurst Island.

GORDON, G. F.—Mate in the *Plover,* (Maguire,) 1850-53. He left the Service after his return in 1854.

Gore, James.—First Lieutenant of the *Resolution,* (Cook,) 1776-79. 1780 succeeded to the command of the *Discovery.* He had served in the expeditions of Byron and Wallis.

GORE, GRAHAM.—Entered the Navy in 1820. A Mate in the *Terror,* (Back,) 1836-37. At the capture of Aden in the *Volage,* in 1839. Mate of the Flag-ship in China, with Sir William Parker. Lieutenant in the *Herald,* (Nias,) in the China war, 1840. First Lieutenant of the *Erebus,* (Franklin,) 1845-47. Landed with a party of men on King William's Island, on May 28th, 1847, and left a record. He died in the winter of 1847-48.

"A man of great stability of character, a very good officer, and the sweetest of tempers, and altogether a capital fellow."—*(Fitzjames.)*

Gore Island, off Southampton Island.

Gore Island, in Queen's Channel.

GRATE, ROBERT.—Boatswain of the *Prince Albert,* (Kennedy,) 1851-52.

GREEN, GEORGE.—Ice Master of the *Terror,* (Back,) 1836-37.

GREGORY, JOHN.—One of the warrant officers of the *Erebus,* (Franklin,) 1845-48.

GREY, H. R. E.—Midshipman in the *Plover,* (Maguire,) in 1853. Volunteered for the *Fox,* (McClintock,) 1857, but could not be spared by their Lordships. Commander, 1870. He passed out at the head of the Class in Nautical Surveying, in the examination of the Royal Naval College, in 1874.

GRIFFITH, W. NELSON.—Entered the Navy in 1811. Midshipman in the *Griper*, (Liddon,) 1819-20. In the Company of the "*Royal Arctic Theatre.*" Acted Captain Loveit, in "*Miss in her Teens;*" Dapper in the "*Citizen;*" Snuffle in the "*Mayor of Garratt;*" Jessamy in "*Bon Ton;*" Sir Philip Modelove in "*Bold stroke for a Wife;*" and Harry in the "*N.W. Passage.*" In the *Hecla*, (Lyon,) 1821-23. Lieutenant in the transport *Barretto Junior*, in 1845, sent to the Whale Fish Islands to fill up Franklin's ships with provisions.

> *Griffith Point*, the south-east point of Melville Island.
> *Griffith Creek*, in Fury and Hecla Strait.

GROVE, JAMES BLAIR.—Mate in the *Assistance*, (Belcher,) 1852-54. Acted Flail in the "*Irish Tutor,*" and Arthur in the "*Silent Woman.*" Commanded an auxiliary sledge party. Afterwards Commander of the Coast Guard at Plymouth, where he died.

HALL, Mr.—Carpenter of the *Enterprise*, (J. C. Ross,) 1848-49, and of the *Resolute*, (Austin,) 1850-51.

HALLETT, J. R.—Clerk in charge of the *Cove*, (J. C. Ross,) 1836. Purser of the *Erebus*, (J. C. Ross,) 1839-43, in the Antarctic Expedition. Afterwards on the Coast of Africa, and died on his way home.

HALSE, JOHN.—Clerk in the *Alexander*, (Parry,) 1818 ; in the *Hecla*, (Parry,) 1819-20. In the Company of the "*Royal Arctic Theatre.*" Acted Will in the "*Citizen*"; Crispin Heeltap in the "*Mayor of Garratt*"; Aminadab in a "*Bold Stroke for a Wife*"; and an Esquimaux in the "*N.W. Passage.*" In the *Fury*, (Parry,) 1821-23; in the *Fury*, (Hoppner,) 1824-25 ; and in the *Hecla*, (Parry,) as Purser, 1827.

> *Cape Halse*, on the east coast of Melville Island.
> *Halse Creek*, in Richards Bay, near Fury and Hecla Strait.

HAMILTON, RICHARD VESEY.—Born at Sandwich. At the Naval School then at Camberwell. Entered the Navy in 1843, in the *Virago* (Mediterranean), and continued to serve on that station until he passed for a mate. Mate in the *Assistance*, (Ommanney,) 1850-51. Prompter and Stage Manager to the Companies of the "*Royal Arctic Theatre*" in 1850-51-53-54. Led one of the auxiliary sledge parties in 1851. Searched Lowther and Young Islands ; 28 days out, and went over

198 miles with Osborn. Lieutenant in the *Resolute*, (Kellett,) 1852-54. In the autumn travelling of 1852, he was away 16 days, and went over 168 miles. In the sledge travelling of 1853 he was 54 days absent from the ship, and went over 675 miles, at an average daily rate of 12 miles. In the winter of 1853-54, he put up the electric telegraph between the *Resolute* and *Intrepid*. 1855, First Lieutenant of the *Desperate* in the Baltic ; 1856, commanding the gun-boat *Haughty* in China, at the battle of Fatshan. Commander, 1856. Captain, 1862. Commanded the Steam Reserve at Devonport, 1873-74. Now Captain Superintendent of Pembroke Dockyard. F.R.G.S. January, 1874, received a good service pension.

Vesey Hamilton Island, off the north point of Sabine Peninsula.

Hamilton Point, on west coast of Prince of Wales' Land.

Harding, Francis.—Lieutenant in the *Griper*, (Lyon,) 1824. Three years in the *Espoir*. Captain, 1841. Now a retired Admiral.

HARRISON, E. N.—Clerk in charge of the *Assistance*, (Ommanney,) 1850-51.

Harvey, William.—Lieutenant in the *Racehorse*, (Phipps,) 1774.

HARWOOD, J.—Junior Engineer in the *Dwarf*, (Lieutenant Sherard Osborn,) 1848-49 ; and behaved so gallantly when that vessel was water-logged off the coast of Ireland, that Lieutenant Osborn applied for him to join the Arctic Expedition of 1850-51. Engineer in the *Pioneer*, (Osborn,) 1850-51 and 1852-54. Acted Mary in the "*Irish Tutor*." Now Chief-Engineer in the *Asia*.

Harwood Island, off the north coast of Bathurst Island.

HASWELL, WILLIAM H.—First Lieutenant of the *Investigator*, (M'Clure,) 1850-54. In the sledge travelling of 1851 he was absent 41 days, from April 18th to May 29th, having explored the west coast of Prince of Wales' Strait. His furthest point was at the entrance of a deep inlet in Wollaston Land, which he reached on May 14th ; and fell in with Esquimaux at the southern entrance of the strait. Now a retired Captain.

Haswell Point, on the west coast of Baring Island.

Hawley, Henry.—Paymaster of the *Phœnix*, (Inglefield,) 1853. Since deceased.

HEAD, H. N.—Midshipman in the *Hecla*, (Parry,) 1824-25. Some of the illustrations in the narrative of Parry's third voyage are from his sketches.

HELPMAN, J. H.—Clerk in charge of the *Terror*, (Crozier,) 1845-48. *Helpman Point*, on the east coast of Wellington Channel.

HENDERSON, J.—Midshipman in the *Fury*, (Parry,) 1821-23. In the Company of the " *Royal Arctic Theatre.*" Acted Bob Acres in the " *Rivals.*"

Point Henderson, on Southampton Island.

HEPBURN, JOHN.—An A.B. in the *Trent*, (Franklin). With Franklin on his land journey of 1819-23 ; " To whom, in the latter part of our journey, we owe the preservation of the lives of some ot our party." *(Franklin's Narrative, p. 88.)* In Van Diemen's Land with Sir John Franklin, filling a civil appointment. Went out in the *Prince Albert*, (Kennedy,) 1851-52, to search for his old Commander. Afterwards received a civil appointment at the Cape of Good Hope, where he died.

HERBERT, F. B.—Mate in the *Assistance*, (Belcher,) 1852-54. In the theatricals of 1852 he acted Terry O'Rourke in the " *Irish Tutor.*" Led an auxiliary party in the sledge travelling of 1853. In 1854 he accompanied Captain Richards on a sledge journey from the *Assistance* to Beechey Island, from the 22nd to the 27th of February, with a temperature of —45 Fahr. Now a retired Commander.

Herbert Point, off the north coast of Bathurst Land.

Hill, J. S.—Master of the *Herald*, (Kellett,) 1845-52. Master of the *Cumberland*, (flag of Sir George Seymour,) West India Station, and was afterwards variously and constantly employed. He died at Aspinwall in 1869.

Hills, Edward H.—Second Master of the *Phœnix*, (Inglefield,) 1853. Late Staff-Commander of the *Agincourt*, (Admiral Hornby,) flag ship of the Channel Squadron, 1871-74.

HOBSON, W. R.—Son of Captain Hobson, the first Governor of New Zealand. Came out to Behring's Straits in the *Rattlesnake*, (Trollope,) 1853 ; and joined the *Plover*, (Maguire). Afterwards in the *Majestic*. Lieutenant in the *Fox*, (McClintock,) 1857-59. In the sledge travelling he was away 74 days, from April 1st to June 14th, 1859, and suffered very severely in health. He was unable to stand on his return. He first discovered the record on King William's Island telling the fate of Franklin. Commander of the *Vigilant* in the East Indies, 1862. Captain, 1866. Now retired.

Hockley, J.—A volunteer in the *Blossom*, (Beechey,) 1825-28.

HODGSON, G. H.—Entered the Navy 1832, and served in the *North Star*, (O. Harcourt,) in the Pacific. Served with distinguished gallantry in the China War in the *Cornwallis*. Lieutenant, 1842. In the *Excellent*, 1844. Second Lieutenant of the *Terror*, (Crozier,) 1845-48.

Cape Hodgson, on the south coast of King William's Island.

Holman, John R., *M.D.*—Assistant-Surgeon of the *Phœnix*, (Ingle-field,) in 1853 and 1854. Now Staff-Surgeon of the *Britannia*, for service on shore, 1872.

HONEY, THOMAS.—Carpenter of the *Terror*, (Crozier,) 1839-43, in the Antarctic Expedition ; and again in the *Terror*, (Crozier,) in the Arctic Expedition, 1845-48.

HOOD, ROBERT.—Mate in Franklin's land journey, 1819. Murdered by the Canadian Michell. Some of the illustrations in the Narrative of Franklin's First Expedition are from his sketches ; and the appendix on the phenomena of the Aurora Borealis.

HOOKER, JOSEPH DALTON.—Assistant-Surgeon in the *Erebus*, (J. C. Ross,) 1839-43, in the Antarctic Expedition. Director of Kew Gardens. President of the Royal Society. C.B., M.D., F.L.S., F.R.G.S.

Author of *" Notes on the Botany of the Antarctic Voyage, conducted by Captain James C. Ross."* (8vo. 1843.)

" Outlines of the Distribution of Arctic Plants." (Trans : Linn : soc : xxiii. p. 251.)

HOOPER, W. H.—Purser of the *Hecla*, (Parry,) 1819-20. In the Company of the *"Royal Arctic Theatre,"* 1819-20. Acted Tag in *" Miss in her Teens "* ; Maria in *" The Citizen"* ; Mrs. Sneak in *" The Mayor of Garratt"* ; Miss Tittup in *" Bon Ton"* ; Mrs. Prim in *" A bold stroke for a Wife"* ; and Susan in *" The N.W. Passage."* Purser of the *Fury*, (Parry,) 1821-23 ; acted Julia in *" The Rivals"* ; of the *Hecla*, (Parry,) 1824-25. Conducted the schools in winter quarters. Afterwards he long held the post of Secretary to Greenwich Hospital. He died on November 8th, 1833.

Hooper Island, in Liddon's Gulf (Melville Island).

Hooper Inlet, near Fury and Hecla Strait.

HOOPER, W. H.—Mate, and afterwards Lieutenant, in the *Plover*, (Moore,) 1849-50. He commanded the *Plover's* cutter in a voyage from Icy Cape to the Mackenzie River. Passed two winters at the Hudson's Bay Company's Stations. He died in 1853, aged 27. F.R.G.S. *See Obituary Notice, R.G.S.J., vol xxiv., p. lxxxiv.* Author of *"Ten months among the Tents of the Tuski."* 1853.

HOPPNER, H. P.—Son of the eminent portrait painter. Lieutenant in the *Alexander*, (Parry,) 1818 ; in the *Griper*, (Liddon,) 1819-20. In the Company of the *" Royal Arctic Theatre."* He acted Jasper in *" Miss in her Teens ;"* Young Wilding in the *" Citizen :"* Jack in the *" N. W. Passage ;"* and Tradelove in a *" Bold stroke for a Wife."* In the *Hecla*, (Lyon,) 1821-23. Acted Fag in the *"Rivals."* Commander of the *Fury*, 1824-25. Got up masquerade balls once a month during winter quarters. Made a land journey of 105 miles from Port Bowen, in June, 1825. He did most of the illustrations for the Narrative of Parry's third voyage. He died at Lisbon in 1833.

> *Cape Hoppner*, on the south shore of Liddon's Gulf.
> *Hoppner Strait*, between Winter Isle and Melville Peninsula.
> *Hoppner Inlet*, in Lyon Inlet, on the coast of Melville Peninsula.
> *Cape Hoppner*, the north point of Cresswell Bay, North Somerset.
> *Cape Hoppner*, between Whale and Booth Sounds, on the Greenland coast.

HORNBY, F.—Mate of the *Terror*, (Crozier,) 1845-48.

> *Hornby Island*, off the west coast of King William's Land.

HULL, THOMAS A.—Master's Assistant in the *Herald*, (Kellett,) 1845-51. Second Master of the *Plover*, (Maguire,) 1852-54, especially charged with the magnetic observations, the results of which were communicated to the Royal Society by General Sabine. (See *Philosophical Transactions, 1857*). Master of the *Havannah*, (Harvey,) 1855-59, when he was presented with a sextant by the Lords of the Admiralty, for surveying services in the Pacific. Senior Assistant-Surveyor of the *Firefly*, (Mansell and Wilkinson,) in the surveys of Palestine, Corfu, and Sicily, 1860-66. Naval Assistant to the Hydrographer, (Richards,) 1866-73, and compiled the wind and current charts, under the direction of Captain Evans ; now Superintendent of Admiralty charts, and Examiner in Nautical Surveying at the Naval College at Greenwich.

Author of *" Practical Nautical Surveying,"* and *" The Unsurveyed World."* *Lectures delivered at the Royal United Service Institution,* (1872).

Hull Point, south of Cape Garry, on the coast of North Somerset.

Hull Point, near Point Barrow.

Hutchinson, John.—Mate in the *Herald*, (Kellett,) 1845-51. Senior Surveyor in the *Herald*, (Sir H Denham,) in the subsequent commission. He remained in Australia, and died as Captain in charge of the South Australian Survey, in 1869.

IBBETT, WILLIAM J.—Second Engineer of the *Intrepid*, (McClintock,) 1852-54. In the sledge travelling he accompanied Mr. McDougall's depôt party across Melville Island. Now chief Engineer of H.M.S. *Minotaur*.

Inglefield, E. A.—Commanded the *Isabel* in 1852, and went to the entrance of Smith Sound during a cruise to Baffin's Bay in the summer. Commanded the *Phœnix*, store ship, in 1853 and 1854, communicating with the *North Star* at Beechey Island ; and brought home part of the Belcher Expedition in 1854. F.R.S., F.R.G.S. (and gold medal), C.B. Now Admiral-Superintendent of Malta Dockyard.

An excellent artist, and author of "*A Summer Search for Sir John Franklin, with a peep into the Polar Basin.*" (1853.)

Inglefield Gulf, the upper part of Whale Sound, in Greenland.

Inman, Lieutenant.—In the *Cove*, (J. C. Ross,) to relieve whalers in 1836.

IRVING, JOHN.—Entered the navy in 1828, and passed in 1834. Served in the *Fly*, (Captain Blackwood,) surveying ship in Australia. Lieutenant in the *Excellent*, 1844. Third Lieutenant of the *Terror*, (Crozier,) 1845-48.

Irving Island, in Queen's Channel.

Irving Island, on the south coast of King William's Island.

Irving, Dr.—Surgeon of the *Racehorse*, (Phipps,) in 1773. Took the meteorological and other observations.

ISEMONGER, J.—Clerk in the *Pagoda* in the Antarctic Expedition of 1845, and assistant in the magnetic observations. He fell from aloft and was drowned at sea in 1846.

JAGO, EDWIN.—Clerk in the *Herald*, (Kellett,) 1845-51. Clerk in charge of the *Plover*, (Maguire,) 1852-54. Now Paymaster of the troop ship *Crocodile*.

JAGO, C. J.—Third Lieutenant of the *Enterprise*, (Collinson,) 1850-54. In the sledge travelling in the spring of 1852 he was away from the ship 49 days. Captain, 1866.

Jenkins, Robert.—Commander of H.M.S. *Talbot.* Came out in 1854 with the *Phœnix*, and brought home part of Belcher's Expedition. Commander of the *Comus*, in China. Captain of the *Actæon*, 1857, and severely wounded during the China war. Captain of the *Miranda* in the New Zealand war. C.B. Good service pension.

JENKINS, ROBERT.—Mate in the *North Star*, (Pullen,) 1853-54; came out in the *Phœnix*, 1853. Retired Commander, 1870.

Jesse, Mr.—Mate in the *Cove*, (J. C. Ross,) in Davies Strait to relieve whalers, 1836.

JOHNSON, Mr.—Boatswain of the *Resolute*, (Kellett,) 1852-54.

KELLETT, HENRY.—Born in November, 1806, and entered the service in 1822. He early took to surveying, and was on the Coast of Africa in the *Ætna*, (Belcher,) 1832-34. In command of the *Starling*, schooner, surveying in the Pacific and China, 1836 to 1842. During the China war he actively co-operated with Collinson in sounding the coast and rivers, and piloting the squadron under Sir William Parker. Captain, 1842, C.B. Captain of the surveying ship *Herald*, 1845-50, surveying the coasts of Central America, the Gulf of California, and Vancouver's Island. In 1848 he went to Norton and Kotzebue Sounds. In July, 1849 he again went to Kotzebue Sound, and took the *Herald* northwards until she was stopped by the ice in 71° 12′ N. He then discovered *Kellett Land*, north of Siberia, and *Herald Island*. He left Behring Strait for the south in October. In July, 1850, he cruised off Cape Lisburne to meet the *Enterprise* and *Investigator*; and eventually left Behring Strait, and returned to England in 1851. In the Arctic Expedition of 1852-54, he was Captain of the *Resolute*, wintering at Dealy Isle (Melville Island). On the Committee of Management of the " *Royal Arctic Theatre*," 1852-54. The plays acted were :—

" *Charles II. ;*"	" *King Glumpus ;*"
" *Who speaks first ;*"	" *Taming the Shrew ;*"
" *Raising the Wind ;*"	" *Two Bonnycastles.*"

Ordered to abandon the *Resolute* by Sir E. Belcher, in May, 1854, and returned home. Afterwards Commodore in the West Indies. Admiral-Superintendent of Malta Dockyard, and Commander-in-Chief on the China Station. K.C.B., F.R.G.S. Retired Vice-Admiral.

Kellett Land, north of the Siberian Coast.
Cape Kellett, the S.W. point of Baring Island.
Kellett Strait, between Eglinton and Melville Islands.

KENDAL, E. N.—Assistant-Surveyor with Lyon in the *Griper,* 1824; Lieutenant, 1825. With Franklin in his second Land Expedition, 1825-27. Some of the illustrations in the Narrative of Franklin's second expedition are from his sketches. Surveyed the coast between the Mackenzie and Copper-mine rivers. Since deceased.

Cape Kendal, near the mouth of the Copper-mine River.

Kendall, J.—Midshipman in the *Blossom,* (Beechey).

KENNEDY, WILLIAM.—Commanded the *Prince Albert,* Lady Franklin's searching vessel, 1851-52. Wintered at Batty Bay, on the west side of Prince Regent's Inlet. In the sledge travelling he left the ship on February 25th, and was at Fury Beach from March 7th to 29th. He discovered Bellot's Strait, marched over Prince of Wales' Land, and round North Somerset, being away 97 days, and covering 1100 miles, with dogs and flat-bottomed Indian sledges.

Author of "*A Short Narrative of the Second Voyage of the Prince Albert.*" (1853.)

KENNEDY, GEORGE.—Boatswain of the *Investigator,* (M'Clure,) 1850-54.

KERR, Mr.—Carpenter of the *Assistance,* (Belcher,) 1852-54.

King, James.—Second Lieutenant of the *Resolution,* (Cooke,) 1776-79. In Cook's third voyage, he succeeded to the command of Captain Clarke's ship on that officer's death in August, 1776.

KING, RICHARD.—Assistant-Surgeon of the *Resolute,* (Austin,) 1850-51.

Kirby, George.—Greenland Master of the *Trent,* (Franklin,) 1818.

KRABBE, FREDERICK J.—Grandson of a Danish officer, taken prisoner in the war. Native of Falmouth and at Greenwich School. Second Master of the *Assistance,* (Ommanney,) 1850-51. Superintended the navigation school for the men in winter quarters. In the company of the "*Royal Arctic Theatre,*" acted Mrs. Honeybun in "*Did you ever send your Wife to Camberwell,*" Phibbs in "*Done on both sides,*" and Triptolemus Muddlewerk in *Charles XII.* Led an auxiliary sledge party to Cape Walker, 13 days away, and went over 116 miles on his first, and 18 days away traversing 110 miles on his second journey. Master of the *Intrepid*, (McClintock,) in 1852-54. Acted Captain Copp in *Charles II.*, and conductor of the conjuring and phantasmagorial entertainments on board the *Intrepid*. In the sledge travelling in 1854 he was 71 days away from the ship, and went over 863 miles. He was in the *Leander* at Balaclava, and in charge of the dockyard at Ascension, 1859-63. Staff-Commander, 1866. Died in 1868.

    Cape Krabbé on the north-east coast of Prince Patrick Island.

Lamont, James.—Of Knockdow, in Argyleshire. A volunteer Arctic explorer. He has made four voyages to Spitzbergen and Novaya Zemlya. Owner of the steam yacht, *Diana*, F.R.G.S. Author of "*Seasons with the Sea Horses*," (1861).

Lane, Mr.—Master of the *Lion*, (Pickersgill,) 1776.

LANE, JOHN.—One of the warrant officers of the *Terror*, (Crozier,) 1845-48.

LANGLEY, Mr.—Boatswain in the *Resolute*, (Austin,) 1850-51.

Law, John.—Surgeon of the *Discovery*, (Clarke,) 1776-80, in Cook's third voyage.

LAWES, WILLIAM.—Clerk of the *Terror*, (Back,) 1836-37.

Lay, Thomas.—Naturalist of the *Blossom*, (Beechey,) 1825-28.
    Lay Point on the American coast, near Icy Cape.

LEASK, JOHN.—An old whaling captain. Ice Master of the *North Star*, (Saunders,) 1849-50, and of the *Prince Albert*, (Kennedy,) 1851-52.

LE VESCONTE, HENRY J. D.—Entered the navy in 1839. In the *Calliope* during the China war, and in the *Clio* with Captain Fitzjames. Second Lieutenant of the *Erebus*, (Franklin,) 1845-48.
    Le Vesconte Point, on Baillie Hamilton Island, in Queen's Channel.
    Point Le Vesconte on the west coast of King William's Island.

Lewis, Charles.—Volunteer in the *Blossom*, (Beechey,) 1825-28.

Lewis, R.—Greenland Pilot in the *Isabella*, (J. Ross,) 1818.

LEWIS, JAMES.—Clerk in the *Resolute*, (Austin,) 1850-51 ; and in the *Assistance*, (Belcher,) 1852-54. Acted Mr. Tillwell in the

Irish Tutor.   Paymaster, 1854.   Appointed in December, 1874, to assist the Arctic Committee in storing and victualling the Arctic Expedition of 1875.

Leyson, William.—Assistant-Surgeon in the *Griper*, (Lyon,) 1824.

LIDDON, MATTHEW.—Entered the navy in 1804 in the *Lily*, in the West Indies.   When in charge of a prize he was captured by a French privateer, and taken into Cumana.   He escaped in the dead of night by swimming off to a schooner with ten of his men.   They captured the schooner after a struggle with the crew, and got away.   At the storming of Monte Video in 1807.   Lieutenant, 1811.   Served in the American War. Lieutenant commanding the *Griper*, 1819-20.   Commander, 1821.   Did not serve afloat afterwards.   Retired Captain, 1856.   He died at Clifton, near Bristol, on August 31st, 1869.

> *Liddon Gulf* on west coast of Melville Island.
> *Liddon Isle* in Fury and Hecla Strait.

LILLY, JOSEPH.—Boatswain of the *Hecla*, (Lyon), 1821-23.

LINDSAY, J. J.—Clerk in charge of the *Plover*, (Moore,) 1848-52.

LITTLE, EDWARD.—Lieutenant, 1837, in the *Vindictive*, (Toup Nicolas,) 1840-44.   First Lieutenant of the *Terror*, (Crozier,) 1845-48.

> *Point Little* on the west coast of King William's Land.

LONEY, J. F.—Master of the *Assistance*, (Belcher,) 1850-54.   Now a retired Staff Captain.

> *Loney Isle* off the north coast of Bathurst Isle.

LUTWIDGE, SKEFFINGTON.—Captain of the *Carcass* in the Spitzbergen voyage, 1773.   Admiral, died 1814.

LYALL, DAVID.—Assistant-Surgeon in the *Terror*, (Crozier,) in the Antarctic Expedition, 1839-43.   Surgeon of the *Assistance*, (Belcher,) 1850-54.   An excellent botanist, and made a valuable collection of the Arctic *flora* about Wellington Channel.   Staff-Surgeon, 1861.   Appointed, December 1874, to assist the Arctic Committee in storing and victualling the expedition of 1875.

> *Lyall Point* on north west of Bathurst Island.

LYON, GEORGE FRANCIS.—Lieutenant, 1814, in the *Berwick*, (Sir E. Pellew).   In the *Albion*, at the battle of Algiers.   Joined Ritchie in the expedition to Tripoli and Mouzouk.   Commander of the *Hecla*, 1821-23.   Manager of the *Royal Arctic Theatre*, 1821-22.   Plays acted :—

" *The Poor Gentleman ;*"   " *The Citizen ;*"
" *Mayor of Garratt ;*"   " *High Life below Stairs ;*"
" *Rowland for an Oliver ;*" " *The Mock Doctor ;*"
" *Raising the Wind ;*"   " *The Heir at Law ;*"
" *The Sleep Walker ;*"   " *The Rivals.*"
" *John Bull ;*"

Captain Lyon acted Captain Absolute in the *Rivals*, and Dick Dowlas in the *Heir at Law*, when he went through the last act with two fingers frost bitten.

Captain of the *Griper*, 1824. In 1825 he married Lucy, daughter of Lord Edward Fitzgerald, who died in 1826. Captain Lyon died in 1832. Author of " *The Private Journal of H.M.S. Hecla during the recent voyage of Discovery,*" (1825). " *Narrative of a voyage to Repulse Bay in H.M.S. Griper,*" (1826). " *Narrative of Travels in Northern Africa in 1818-20, with Geographical notices of Soudan.*" (1821). " *Journal of a Tour in Mexico, in 1826.*" 2 vols. (1828). Captain Lyon was also an artist, and drew all the sketches which illustrate the narrative of Parry's second voyage.

Lyon Inlet in the south part of Melville Peninsula, near Repulse Bay.

Lyons, Israel.—Lieutenant and Astronomer in the *Racehorse*, (Phipps,) 1774.

Mac Bean, C. A.—Second Master in the *Terror*, (Crozier,) 1845-48.

McClintock, Francis Leopold.—Son of Mr. H. McClintock, of the 3rd Dragoon Guards. Born at Dundalk in 1819. Entered the Navy, 1831. Mate in the *Gorgon*, (Sir C. Hotham,) and Lieutenant in the *Frolic* brig in the Pacific, 1845-47. Second Lieutenant of the *Enterprise*, (J. C. Ross,) 1848-49. In the sledge travelling he left the ship, with Sir James Ross, on May 15th, and reached the furthest point on June 5th, examining the north and west shores of North Somerset. Away from the ship 40 days, and went over 500 miles, a feat unprecedented at that time. First Lieutenant of the *Assistance*, (Ommanney,) 1850-51. Commander of the *Intrepid*, 1850-54, Captain of the *Fox* in Lady Franklin's expedition, 1857-59. In Captain Austin's expedition he took the lead in the organization of the sledge travelling. In 1850 he made a journey from October 2nd to 9th, to lay out a depôt. In 1851, he started April 15th and returned July 4th, travelling from Griffith Island to Melville Island ; away 80 days and travelled over 770 miles, at a daily rate of 10½ miles. In Captain Kellett's Expedition he

brought the system of sledge travelling to still greater per-
fection. In 1852 he was away in the autumn for 40 days,
laying out a depôt, and went over 225 miles. In 1853 he
was away 105 days, and travelled 1328 miles at a daily rate
of 12·7 miles. In his *Fox* expedition he began depôt
travelling on the 17th February until 14th March. *Temp.*
—40 to —48. Later in 1859 he was away 90 days, and
marched round King William's Island, and to the mouth of
the Great Fish River, discovering the fate of Franklin,
and finally solving the question of the fate of the officers and
crews of the *Erebus* and *Terror.* Captain, 1854. Knighted,
1859. L.L.D. (Dublin), F.R.S., F.R.G.S., D.C.L., *Gold
Medal* R.G.S., 1860. Now Admiral-Superintendent of Portsmouth Dockyard. Appointed in December, 1874, (with
Admirals Richards and Osborn,) to form a Committee to
assist in the organization of the Arctic Expedition of 1875.
Author of " *Reminiscences of Arctic Ice Travel*" (for the Journal
of the Dublin Society, 1857). " *The Voyage of the Fox in the
Arctic Seas.*" (1859.)

McClintock Channel, between Prince Albert and Prince of
Wales' Land.

Cape McClintock, north point of Prince Patrick Land.

Cape McClintock, north shore of North Somerset.

McClintock Land, south of Zichy Land (Austrian discoveries).

M'CLURE, ROBERT JOHN LE MESURIER.—Was born at Wexford in
1807. He entered the navy in 1816. Mate in the *Terror,*
(Back,) 1836-37. Lieutenant, 1838, serving on the Canada
Lakes. First Lieutenant of the *Pilot* in the West Indies,
1839-42. Commanded the *Romney,* receiving ship at
Havanna, 1842-46. First Lieutenant of the *Enterprise,* (J.
C. Ross,) 1848-49. Commander of the *Investigator,*
1850-54. He wintered, in 1850-51, off the Princess Royal
Isles in Prince of Wales' Strait ; and was away travelling
to the north from October 21st to 31st, 1850. *On October
26th, 1850, he sighted Melville Island, and so discovered a
North West Passage.* On May 30th, 1851, owing to a report
from Lieutenant Haswell, he set out with Mr. Miertching,
the interpreter, to communicate with Esquimaux to the south,
returning on June 4th. In 1851, the *Investigator* passed
round Banks' Island and wintered in the Bay of Mercy. In
the spring of 1852 M'Clure made a journey to Winter
Harbour in Melville Island from April 11th to May 11th, and
left a record which was found in the autumn by Lieutenant
Mecham *(whom see).* In the spring of 1852 the *Investigator*

was abandoned, and M'Clure, with the officers and crew, came over to the *Resolute* at Melville Island. M'Clure returned to England 1854, and his Captain's commission was dated October 26th, 1854, the day of his great discovery. *Knighted.* F.R.G.S., and Gold Medal of 1854. Parliament granted the reward of £10,000 to M'Clure, his officers, and crew, in consideration of their having been the first to pass from the Pacific to the Atlantic Oceans by the Arctic Sea. Captain of H.M.S. *Esk* in China, 1856-61. C.B. for the capture of Canton. Retired Vice-Admiral. He died October 17th, 1873, aged 66. See " *The Discovery of a North-West Passage by H.M.S :*" ' *Investigator,*' *Captain M'Clure, during the years 1850-54, Edited by Captain Sherard Osborn, C.B., Royal Navy, from the Logs and Journals of Captain M'Clure,* (four editions). See also *Obituary Notice of Sir R. M'Clure. Ocean Highways. December, 1873, p. 353.*

M'Clure Bay, on the north coast of North Somerset.
Cape M'Clure, on the north coast of Bank's Island.
M'Clure Strait, south of Prince of Wales' Strait.

MAC DIARMID, G.—Surgeon of the *Victory,* (Ross,) 1829-33.

MACDONALD, A.—Went for a voyage up Baffin's Bay with Captain Penny in 1839. Author of " *Enakooapik, or the Discovery of Penny's Gulf.*" Assistant-Surgeon of the *Terror,* (Crozier,) 1845-48.

M'CORMICK, ROBERT.—Assistant-Surgeon in the *Hecla,* (Parry,) 1827. Surgeon and Naturalist of the *Erebus,* (J. C. Ross,) in the Antarctic Expedition, 1839-43. Went out in the *Assistance,* (Belcher,) 1852, to make a boat expedition up the coast of Wellington Channel. He started from Beechey Island on August 19, and returned September 8th to the *North Star.* He returned home in the *Phœnix* in 1853. Author of " *Narrative of a boat expedition up the Wellington Channel in 1852, in H.M.B. Forlorn Hope* (1854). Now a retired Deputy-Inspector of Hospitals and Fleets.

M'Cormick Bay on the east coast of Wellington Channel.

MAC DOUGALL, GEORGE F.—At Greenwich School. Master's Assistant in the *Samarang,* (Belcher). Second Master in the *Resolute,* (Austin,) 1850-51. Editor of the " *Illustrated Arctic News,*" jointly with Sherard Osborn. In the company of the " *Royal Arctic Theatre.*" Acted Erica in *Charles XII.* In the sledge travelling he started first on April 4th, and was away 20 days, going over 140 miles. In a second journey he traversed 198 miles in 20 days. Master of the *Resolute,*

(Kellett,) 1852-54. On the Committee of Management of the "*Royal Arctic Theatre.*" Acted Mary in *Charles II.* Instructor of a class in navigation. In the sledge travelling of 1853 he led a depôt party across Melville Island for Hamilton's extended party, and was away from April 27th to May 6th, travelling over 205 miles. In the winter of 1853-54 he read a series of papers to the men on Arctic Exploration. In 1856 he was surveying the west coast of Ireland. In 1858 surveying the coast of Ceylon. Staff-Commander, 1866. Naval Assistant in the Hydrographic Department of the Admiralty. F.R.G.S. He died suddenly in 1870. He was an excellent artist, draughtsman, and nautical surveyor.

Author of "*The Eventful Voyage of H.M.S. Resolute to the Arctic Regions,*" (1857).

Mc Dougall Bay between Bathurst and Cornwallis Islands.

Mc Dougall Point on the north west coast of Sabine Peninsula.

Mac Innes, A.—Second Engineer of the *Victory*, (Ross), 1829-33.

Macklin, Joseph.—Gunner of the *Hecla*, (Lyon,) 1821-23.

Mac Laren, A.—Assistant-Surgeon of the *Hecla*, (Lyon,) in 1821-23.

Cape Mac Loren, the west entrance to Lyon Inlet, on the coast of Melville Peninsula.

Mac Murdo, Archibald.—Third Lieutenant of the *Terror*, (Back,) 1836-37. First Lieutenant of the *Terror*, (Crozier,) 1839-43, in the Antarctic Expedition. Invalided from the Falkland Islands, after the second voyage south. Retired Rear-Admiral, 1867.

Point Mac Murdo off Southampton Island.

Maguire, Rochfort.—Entered the navy in 1830. Served on the coast of Syria in the *Wasp*, and was severely wounded on the head, at the capture of Sidon. Lieutenant in the *Vernon*, (Walpole,) 1841-44. First Lieutenant of the *Herald*, (Kellett,) 1845-51. Commander of the *Plover*, 1852-54, during her two winters at Point Barrow. "*The narrative of Commander Maguire wintering at Point Barrow,*" is printed as an Appendix to Sherard Osborn's, "*The Discovery of a North West Passage by Captain M'Clure.*" Captain Maguire afterwards commanded the *Sanspariel*, *Imperieuse*, and *Galatea*, and was Commodore on the Australian Station. He was invalided and died at Haslar in 1867. C.B., F.R.G.S.

Cape Maguire on the north west shore of Boothia.

D

Manico, Peter S.—Entered the Navy in 1806, in the *Ocean*, (Lord Collingwood) ; and served in the war on the coast of Catalonia. First Lieutenant of the *Griper*, (Lyon,) 1824, but did not serve afloat afterwards.

MANN, EDWARD.—Boatswain in the *Terror*, (Crozier,) 1839-43, in the Antarctic Expedition. In the *Dædolus*, (McQuay,) 1848. Died at Woolwich, 1849.

MANSON, MR.—Mate in the *Sophia*, (Stewart,) 1850-51 ; in the *Isabel*, (Inglefield,) 1852, and in the *Phœnix*, (Inglefield,) 1853 and 1854.

    Manson Isle, off the entrance of Wolstenholme Sound, (Greenland).

MARKHAM, CLEMENTS R.—Entered the Navy 1844, in the *Collingwood*, (Flag of Sir George Seymour,) in the Pacific, 1844-48. Midshipman in the *Assistance*, (Ommanney,) 1850-51. Editor of " *The Minavilins*," an Arctic newspaper. In the company of the " *Royal Arctic Theatre.*" Acted Fusbos in " *Bombastes Furioso*," and Gustavus de Mervelt in " *Charles XII.*" In the sledge travelling with McDougall's and May's exploring parties, away altogether 40 days. With McDougall he was away 20 days, and marched over 140 miles, starting on April 4th (Temperature —31 Fahr.) returning April 24th. 1852 left the service. C.B. Commendador of the Order of Christ. Chevalier of the Order of the Rose of Brazil. F.R.S., F.L.S., F.S.A., Sec. R.G.S. since 1863. Secretary of the Hakluyt Society since 1858. Author of " *Franklin's Footsteps*," (1853,) " *The Threshold of the Unknown Region*," (1873. 3rd edition, 1875,) of articles in the *Quarterly Review*, (July, 1865,) *Contemporary Review*, (October, 1873,) and other periodicals, advocating the despatch of an Arctic Expedition ; and of papers on the " *Origin and Migrations of the Greenland Esquimaux*," on " *The Arctic Highlanders*," and on " *Discoveries East of Spitzbergen*," &c., in the R.G.S.J.

    Markham Island, off the north point of Sabine Peninsula.

    Markham Point, on west coast of MacDougall Bay.

    Clements Markham Bay, south of Cape Garry in North Somerset.

    Markham Sound, between McClintock and Zichy Land, (Austrian discoveries).

Markham, Albert H.—Cousin of the above. He entered the navy in 1856. Served in China 1856 to 1864, during the war. Lieutenant, 1862, for his " gallant conduct in capturing a pirate vessel." Lieutenant of the *Victoria*, in the

Mediterranean, 1864-67. First Lieutenant of the *Blanche,* on the Australian Station, 1868-71. Acting Commander of the *Rosario* cruising among the Santa Cruz and New Hebrides groups, 1871. Commander, 1872. Went for a voyage in the whaler *Arctic,* (Captain Adams,) up Baffin's Bay and Prince Regent's Inlet, 1873. F.R.G.S. Commander in H.M.S. *Sultan,* 1873-74. Author of " *A Whaling Cruise in Baffin's Bay,*" (1874,) and " *The Cruise of the Rosario,*" (1873). Appointed to the Arctic Expedition of 1875, on December 8th, 1874.

MARCUARD, CHARLES.—Mate in the *Terror,* (Back,) 1836-37.

Marsh, George.—Purser of the *Blossom,* (Beechey,) 1825-28.

MARTIN, H.—Second Master of the *Plover,* (Moore,) 1848-50. In Maguire's boat expedition to Point Barrow, 1850. Died at Southampton in 1853.

MATTHIAS, H.—Assistant-Surgeon in the *Enterprise.* (J. C. Ross,) 1848. Died in winter quarters at Port Leopold, on June 15th, 1849, aged 27.

MAY, WALTER WALLER.—Mate in the *Resolute,* (Austin,) 1850-51. Acted Colonel Reichel in *Charles XII.* In the travelling led one of the depôt parties as far as Cape Gillman on Bathurst Island, 34 days away and marched 371 miles, and a short exploring party, round Griffith Island. Lieutenant of the *Assistance,* (Belcher,) 1852-54. Scene painter to the " *Queen's Arctic Theatre.*" In the travelling he was away 62 days, going over 600 miles, at a daily rate of 10 miles. Retired Commander, 1854. He published a series of sketches of scenes during the voyage of the *Assistance,* 1855. The illustrations in M'Clintock's " *Voyage of the Fox,*" are from his drawings. Now an eminent watercolour artist. The bas-relief on the pedestal of Franklin's statue, in Waterloo Place, is from his design.

May Inlet on the north shore of Bathurst Island.

Meara, Edward S.—A Lieutenant in the *Phœnix,* (Inglefield,) 1854. A retired Captain of October, 1873.

MECHAM, FREDERICK G.—Was born at the Cove of Cork in 1828. Entered the navy in 1841 on board the *Ardent* (Captain Russell,) hence the name of Russell Island to his discovery. Midshipman in the *Constance,* in the Pacific, 1846-48. Second Lieutenant in the *Assistance,* (Ommanney,) 1850-51. In the autumn sledge-travelling he was away from October 2nd to 7th, and discovered the winter quarters of Penny's brigs. In the company of the *Royal Arctic Theatre,* acted Mr. Honeybun in "*Did you ever send your Wife to Camberwell*," Brown-john in "*Done on both Sides*," and "*Charles XII.*" In the sledge travelling of 1851 Mecham was away 28 days, went over 236 miles, and discovered Russell Island. First Lieutenant of the *Resolute*, (Kellett,) 1852-54. In the company of the "*Royal Arctic Theatre*," of 1852-53. Acted Charles II. in the historical drama of that name. In the autumn travelling of 1852 he was away 23 days, and went over 184 miles. He discovered the record left by M'Clure at Winter Harbour. In the travelling of 1853 he was away 94 days, and went over 1163 miles, at a daily rate of 12½ miles. In 1854 he was away 71 days, and went over 1336 miles, at the extraordinary rate of 16 miles a day on the outward, and 20½ on the homeward journey. Commander 1855. Appointed to the *Vixen* in the Pacific 1857, and died of bronchitis at Honolulu in February, 1858. F.R.G.S.

[See *Obituary Notice, R.G.S.J., vol. xxix., p. xxxiii.*]

Cape Mecham, south point of Prince Patrick Land.

Mecham Island in the strait between Russell and Prince of Wales' Islands.

MIERTCHING, JOHN.—A Moravian Missionary. Eskimo Inter-preter to the *Investigator*, (McClure,) 1850-54.

MOGG, WILLIAM.—Clerk in the *Hecla*, (Lyon,) 1821-23. Acted Lucy in the *Rivals*. In the *Fury*, (Hoppner,) 1824-25. Conducted the schools during the winter.

Mogg Bay in Hooper Inlet, near Fury and Hecla Strait.

MOORE, T. E. L.—Entered the navy in 1832. Mate in the *Terror*, (Crozier,) 1839-43, in the Antarctic Expedition. Commanded the *Pagoda* in the Antarctic Expedition of 1845, to complete the magnetic observations, with Captain (now General,) Clerk, R.E. Commander of the *Plover*, 1848-50. Led a boat expedition to Point Barrow, 1850. Afterwards Governor of the Falkland Islands from 1855 to 1862. Rear-Admiral. F.R.S. He died in 1870.

MOORE, L. J.—Midshipman in the *Fisgard*, (Duntz,) in the Pacific, 1842-46. Mate in the Investigator (Bird,) 1848-49. Now a retired Captain.

Moore, John.—Master's Assistant in the *Plover*, but returned to England in the *Herald*.

MOORE, JOHN.—Gunner in the *Fury*, (Hoppner,) 1824-25.

Morrell, Arthur.—Entered the navy 1801, and served in the West Indies for nine years. Lieutenant in the *Dorothea*, (Buchan,)

1818, in the Spitzbergen voyage. Nearly broke his heart for want of employment. 1844 in command of the *Tortoise* at Ascension until 1846, when he was unfairly superseded.

MOUBRAY, GEO. H.—Entered the service in 1828. Clerk in charge of the *Terror*, (Crozier,) 1839-43, in the Antarctic Expedition. Naval Agent and Storekeeper at Constantinople during the Crimean War. Storekeeper at Malta, 1862 to 1870. Now retired with the rank of Paymaster-in-Chief, and awarded the Greenwich Pension.

MOULD, JOHN A.—Entered the navy as Assistant-Surgeon in 1827. Served in the *Lightning*, in the operations at the wreck of the *Thetis*, at Cape Frio. 1835, Acting Surgeon of the *Challenger*, (Seymour,) when she was wrecked on the coast of Chile. Seven weeks under canvass. Assistant-Surgeon in the *Terror*, (Back,) 1836-37. Surgeon, 1838, of the *Phœnix*, during the Syrian war. Served at Malta as Surgeon of the *Ceylon* and *Hibernia*, for ten years, 1851-61. Now a retired Deputy Inspector of Hospitals.

NARES, GEORGE S.—Mate in the *Resolute*, (Kellett,) 1852-54. Acted Lady Clara in the historical drama of "*Charles II,*" and in the second winter read papers, with diagrams, on the laws of mechanics, and on winds. In the autumn travelling of 1852, he was away 25 days, and went over 186 miles. In the sledge travelling, commanded Mecham's auxilliary party in 1853, and went over 665 miles in 60 days. In 1854 he was away 55 days in extreme cold (March) and went over 586 miles. Lieutenant, 1854. First Lieutenant of the *Britannia*, training ship for Naval Cadets. Commander of the *Salamander*, surveying in Torres Strait, and inside the Barrier Reef, 1865-66. Surveyed the coasts of Sicily and Tunis, and the gulf of Suez in the *Newport* and *Shearwater*. Captain, 1869, of the exploring ship *Challenger*, 1872-74. F.R.G.S. Author of a work on *Seamanship* (250 pages and 400 woodcuts), 8vo. *(5th edition).* December, 9th, 1874 appointed to command the Arctic Expedition of 1875.

Cape Nares, S.W. point of Eglinton Island.

Nelson, Horatio.—Born 1758. In the *Carcass*, (Lutwidge,) 1818, in the Spitzbergen voyage, having entered as Captain's Coxswain, in the absence of an officer's vacancy. Lieutenant, 1777. Captain, 1779. Baron Nelson of the Nile, Viscount Nelson, Duke of Bronte. K.B. Fell at Trafalgar, October 21st, 1805.

Nelson Island, one of the Seven Islands, off the north coast of Spitzbergen.

Nelson, T.—Surgeon of the *Blossom*, (Beechey,) 1825-28.

NEILL, S.—Surgeon in the *Hecla*, (Parry,) 1824-25. An able and accomplished naturalist.

> *Port Neill*, south of Port Bowen, on the east coast of Prince Regent's Inlet.

NIAS, JOSEPH.—Entered the Navy in 1807. Midshipman in the *Alexander*, (Parry,) 1818; in the *Hecla*, (Parry,) 1819-20. In the company of the "*Royal Arctic Theatre*," in 1819-20. He acted Sir Simon Loveit in "*Miss in her Teens*"; Sir Joseph Wilding in the "*Citizen*"; Sir Jacob Jollup in the "*Mayor of Garratt*"; Tom in the "*N. W. Passage*"; Davy in "*Bon Ton*"; and Periwinkle in "*A bold stroke for a Wife.*" Accompanied Parry in the journey across Melville Island. Lieutenant, 1820; in the *Fury*, (Parry,) 1821-23. At the battle of Navarino. Captain, 1835; of the *Herald* during the China war, 1838-43. C.B., 1841. Rear-Admiral, 1857. Retired-Admiral, 1867. K.C.B.

> *Nias Point*, on the south shore of Hecla and Griper Bay.
> *Nias Islands*, at the entrance of Duke of York Bay, at the north end of Southampton Island.

NORMAN, M.—Second Master in the *North Star*, (Saunders,) 1849-50.

OAKELEY, HENRY.—Mate in the *Erebus*, (J. C. Ross,) 1838-43, in the Antarctic Expedition. Retired Commander since 1864.

OMMANNEY, ERASMUS.—Entered the Navy in 1826. Lieutenant in the *Pique*, (Rous,) in the West Indies. Lieutenant in the *Cove*, (J. C. Ross,) 1836, in Davis Straits, in search of missing whalers, in the depth of winter. Commander, 1840; of the *Vesuvius*, in the Mediterranean, 1841-44. Captain, 1846. Rendered valuable service in Ireland, during the famine. Captain of the *Assistance*, 1850-51. Manager of the "*Royal Arctic Theatre.*" The plays acted were

"*Did you ever send your Wife to Camberwell;*"	"*Bombastes Furioso;*"
	"*Charles XII;*"
"*Done on both sides;*"	"*High life below stairs;*"
"*The Lottery Ticket;*"	"*Zero, or Harlequin Light.*"

He acted Mrs. Crank in "*Did you ever send your Wife to Camberwell*," and Vanberg in "*Charles XII.*" In the sledge travelling he explored a part of Prince of Wales' Land, away 60 days, and went over 480 miles. In 1854 he had the *Eurydice*, and commanded the squadron in the White Sea; in 1855 the *Hawk* in the Baltic. 1864, Rear-Admiral. 1874, Retired-Admiral. C.B., F.R.S., F.R.G.S.

> *Ommanney Bay*, in Prince of Wales' Land.

OSBORN, SHERARD.—Midshipman in the *Hyacinth*, (Warren,) in China, at the capture of Canton in 1841. Gunnery Mate and Lieutenant in the *Collingwood* (Flag of Sir George Seymour) in the Pacific, 1844-48. Lieutenant commanding the *Dwarf*, on the coast of Ireland, 1849. Lieutenant commanding the *Pioneer* in 1850-51. In the winter he was joint Editor, with MacDougall, of the "*Illustrated Arctic News*." In the sledge travelling in 1851, he went to the furthest western point of Prince of Wales' Land, away from his ship 58 days, and travelled over 534 miles. Commander, 1852; of the *Pioneer*, 1852-54. Manager of the "*Arctic Philharmonic Entertainments*" on board the *Pioneer*. In the sledge travelling of 1853 he was away 117 days, and went over 1093 miles. In 1855 he was in the *Vesuvius*, and commanded the advanced squadron in the Sea of Azoff. Captain, 1855. C.B., and Officer *Legion of Honour* and *Medjidie*. 1857, in the *Furious*, and shared in all the operations of the second Chinese war. Took the *Furious* up the Yang-tsze to Hankow, in 1858. Rear-Admiral, 1873. F.R.S., F.R.G.S., F.L.S. Chevalier of the Order of the Rose of Brazil. Author of "*Stray Leaves from an Arctic Journal*," (1852,) and Editor of M'Clure's "*Narrative of the Discovery of the North West Passage*," (1855). Author of "*The Career, Last Voyage, and Fate of Sir John Franklin*," (1860). Read papers urging the renewal of Polar Exploration before the Geographical Society, on January 23rd, 1865, and in January, 1872. Appointed in December, 1874, on a Committee (with Admirals Sir L. McClintock and Richards,) to make preparations for the Arctic Expedition of 1875.

Sherard Osborn Isle, off north coast of Bathurst Island.

Cape Sherard Osborn, on west coast of Prince of Wales' Land.

Cape Sherard Osborn, at south entrance of Lancaster Sound.

Cape Sherard Osborn, on Crown Prince Rudolph Land, (Austrian discoveries).

OSBORN, NOEL.—Came out in the *Phœnix*, (Inglefield,) 1853; and was a mate in the *North Star*, 1853-54. Retired Captain, 1873. He died on January 23rd, 1875.

OSMER, CHARLES H.—In the *Blossom*, (Beechey,) 1825-28, and served afterwards on the Canadian Lakes. Purser of the *Erebus*, (Franklin,) 1845-48.

> "Merry hearted as any young man, full of quaint dry sayings, always good humoured, always laughing, never a bore."—*(Fitzjames.)*

Osmer Bay, on the east coast of Bathurst Island.

Oyston, Mr.— Mate in the *Isabel*, (Inglefield,) 1852.

Pakenham, Robert E.—Midshipman in the *Herald*, (Kellett,) 1845-51. Afterwards left the service.

PAINE, J. C.—Clerk in charge of the *Investigator*, (M'Clure,) 1852-54. Now a retired Paymaster.

PALMER, C.—Lieutenant in the *Hecla*, (Lyon,) 1821-23. He had been a Mate in the *Dorothea*, (Buchan,) 1818. He did not serve after 1823.

  Palmer Bay, on east coast of Melville Peninsula.

PARKES, M. T.—Mate in the *Enterprise*, (Collinson,) 1852-54. In the sledge travelling of 1852 he left the ship April 16th, and travelled up Prince of Wales' Strait. He reached Melville Island on foot, having had to leave sledge and tent owing to the ice being too rough to drag the sledge. Returned to the sledge after an absence of 11 days, some of the crew suffering severely from frost bites. Got back to the ship on June 28th, having been away 74 days. Now a retired Commander.

PARRY, W. EDWARD.—Third son of Dr. C. Parry, of Bath, where he was born in 1790. He entered the navy on board the *Ville de Paris*, (Ricketts,) in 1803. First Lieutenant of the *Niger*, 1815. Lieutenant commanding the *Alexander* 1818, and the *Hecla*, 1819-20, in command of the expedition. Sailed through Barrow Strait and discovered Melville Island. In the company of the "*Royal Arctic Theatre*," in 1819-20. Acted Fribble, in *Miss in her Teens*"; Old Philpot in the "*Citizen*"; Matthew Mug in the "*Mayor of Garratt*"; Sir John Trotley in "*Bon Ton*"; and Bill, in the "*North West Passage.*" Made a journey across Melville Island, June 1st to 15th, 1820. Commander of the *Fury*, 1821-23, and in command of the expedition. Acted Sir Anthony Absolute in the "*Rivals.*" Discovered the passage into the Polar Sea by the "Fury and Hecla Strait." 1823, Acting Hydrographer. Captain of the *Hecla*, 1824-25, and commanding the expedition. 1826, Acting Hydrographer. 1827, Captain of the *Hecla* in the attempt to reach the Pole. Attained 82°, 45′ N. Lat. on July 23, having travelled 172 miles from the *Hecla*. Went over 580 miles of ground. Hydrographer from 1827 to 1829. Commissioner of the Australian Agricultural Company of New South Wales, 1829-34. Comptroller of Steam Machinery 1837 to 1846. Captain Superintendent of Haslar, 1846 to 1852. He died at Ems on July 8th, 1853, and was interred at Greenwich. F.R.S., D.C.L., F.R.G.S. (*Original Member*). *Knighted, April*

29th, 1829. Author of "*Journal of a Voyage to discover a North West Passage, 1819-20*" (1821); of "*Journal of a second Voyage,*" *&c.* (1824) ; *of* "*Journal of a third voyage*" (1826); and of "*Narrative of an attempt to reach the North Pole*" (1828) ; all 4to. [*See Obituary Notice, R.G.S.J.,* vol. *xxvi., p. clxxxii.*] This notice was written by Admiral Beechey, the great explorer's old messmate in the *Niger,* and friend. See also a Memoir of Sir Edward Parry, (1857,) by his son, the Rev. Edward Parry, now Suffragan Bishop of Dover. *Memoirs of Rear-Admiral Sir Edward Parry, Knight, late Lieutenant-Governor of Greenwich Hospital, by his son the Rev. Edward Parry, M.A., (3rd edition, Longman, 1857).*

The Parry Islands consist of Prince Patrick, Melville, Bathurst and Cornwallis Islands ; and many smaller isles.

Parry Island off the north coast of Spitzbergen.

Cape Parry, between Whale and Booth Sounds (Greenland.)

Cape Parry on the American coast, east of the mouth of Mackenzie.

Parsons, W. F.—Second Master of the *Herald,* (Kellett,) 1846-50. Master of the *Herald,* (Denham,) in the subsequent commission. Now retired.

Peard, George.—Eldest son of Vice-Admiral Shuldham Peard. Born at Gosport in 1793. Entered the navy, 1805. First Lieutenant of the *Blossom,* (Beechey,) 1825-28. He died from the effects of climate in 1837.

PEARSE, RICHARD BULKELEY.—Entered the navy in the *Winchester,* at the Cape, 1842-45, afterwards in the *Constance,* in the Pacific, 1846-49. Mate in the *Resolute,* (Austin,) 1850-51. Acted Lydia in "*Done on Both Sides,*" and Ulrica in *Charles XII.* Led an auxiliary sledge party to provision Lieutenant Aldrich, as far as Cape Cockburn on Bathurst Island, 24 days away, and marched 208 miles. Severely frost-bitten and eventually lost a leg, for which he receives a pension. Now a retired Captain. F.R.G.S.

Pearse Inlet, on the west coast of Bathurst Island.

Peckover, William.—Gunner in the *Discovery,* (Clarke,) 1776-80, in Cook's expedition.

PEDDIE, J. S.—Surgeon of the *Terror,* (Crozier,) 1845-48.

PENNY, WILLIAM.—An experienced whaling Captain, placed in command of two brigs, the *Lady Franklin* and *Sophia,* 1850-51.

Explored part of the shore of Wellington Channel. Now living at Aberdeen.

Penny Strait, north of Queen's Channel.

PETERSEN, CARL.—A Dane of Greenland. Eskimo Interpreter to Penny, 1850-51, to Kane, 1852-54, and to McClintock, 1857-59. Rewarded with the charge of a light-house in Denmark.

Petersen Point, on the west coast of Wellington channel.

PHAYRE, G. A.—First Lieutenant of the *Enterprise*, (Collinson,) 1850-54. Now a retired Captain.

Philips, Molesworth.—Lieutenant of Marines in the *Resolution*, (Cook,) 1776-79.

Phillips, Joshua.—Greenland Master in the *Isabella*, (Ross,) 1818.

PHILLIPS, CHARLES G.—Entered the navy in 1820. Second Lieutenant of the *Terror*, (Crozier,) in the Antarctic Expedition, 1839-42. Second to Sir John Ross in the *Felix*, 1850-51. Made a land journey over Cornwallis Island. He died in 1872.

Cape Phillips at the north end of Cornwallis Island.

Phipps, Constantine John.—Son of the First Lord Mulgrave. Entered the Navy. Captain of the *Racehorse*, 1773, in the Spitzbergen voyage, and commanding the Expedition. In 1787 he married Anne, daughter of N. Cholmley, of Howsham. He succeeded as second Lord Mulgrave in 1774 ; and died in 1792. He was the Author of "*Arctic Voyage towards the North Pole, 1773.*" (4to. 1774.)

Phipps Island, one of the Seven Islands, off the north coast of Spitzbergen.

Pickersgill, Richard.—Lieutenant commanding the *Lion*, brig, 1776, sent to meet Cook by way of Baffin's Bay. He did not get beyond Davis Strait.

PICTHORN, T. R.—Assistant-Surgeon in the *Pioneer*, (Osborn,) 1850-51. Now Deputy-Inspector of Hospitals.

PIERS, HENRY.—Assistant-Surgeon in the *Investigator*, (M'Clure,) 1850-54. Now a retired Deputy-Inspector of Hospitals.

PIM, BEDFORD P. T.—Born in 1826, entered the navy in 1842, and served under Captain Sheringham, surveying the south coast of England. Midshipman in the *Herald*, (Kellett,) 1845-48. In the *Plover*, (Moore,) 1848-49. Made a land journey from Kotzebue Sound to Norton Sound. Lieutenant, 1851. Went to St. Petersburg to propose a search for Franklin along the Siberian coast, which was declined. Lieutenant in the *Resolute*, (Kellett,) 1852-54. Acted Edward (a page) in " *Charles II.*" In the sledge travelling he was away 17 days in the autumn, and went over 175 miles. In the spring he was sent to communicate with the *Investigator* on March 10th and returned April 19th, 1853. He was away 41 days, and travelled 427 miles. He made another journey of 20 days going over 123 miles. Commanded the *Magpie*, gunboat, in the Baltic, and the *Banterer*, gun boat, in China, 1857-58, and severely wounded in the Canton river. Commander, 1858. Commanded H.M.S. *Gorgon* in the West India Station, 1858-60, and the *Fury*, on the coast of Africa, 1860-61. Obtained a concession from the King of Mosquito for a railway, and has been four times to Nicaragua on business connected with the project, 1863-64-65-66. Now a retired Captain. M.P. for Gravesend. J.P. F.R.G.S. He is author of " *An Earnest Appeal to the British Public on behalf of the Missing Arctic Expedition*," (1857,) and " *The Gate of the Pacific.*" Captain Pim was called to the Bar in 1873. He is proprietor of the " Navy," newspaper.

PORTEUS, A.—Surgeon in the *Felix*, (J. Ross,) 1850-51.

PULLEN, W. J. S.—In the *Columbia* surveying on the North American Station, 1844-48, with Captain Shortland. Lieutenant, 1846, of the *Plover*, (Moore,) 1848-50. Commanded the boat expedition between Behring Strait and the Mackenzie river. Commander, 1850. Ascended the river Mackenzie to the Great Slave Lake, 1849-50. Commander of the *North Star*, at Beechey Island, 1852-54. Captain of the *Cyclops* in the Red Sea, sounding for the electric telegraph ; and employed in the survey of Bermuda. Now a retired Captain.

PULLEN, T. C.—Master in the *North Star*, (Pullen,) 1852-54. Master Attendant, 1864-72. Now a retired Staff-Captain.

PURCHASE, THOMAS R.—Second Engineer in the *Intrepid*, (Cator,) 1850-51, and in the *Intrepid*, (McClintock,) 1852-54. *Purchase Bay*, west coast of Melville Island.

PURFUR, C.—Carpenter in the *Hecla*, (Lyon,) 1821-23 ; in the *Fury*, (Hoppner,) 1824-25.

PYM, F. W.—Mate in the *Assistance*, (Belcher,) 1852-54.

RAE, JAMES.—Assistant-Surgeon in the *North Star*, (Saunders,) 1849-50. Now a retired Deputy Inspector of Hospitals.

REID, ANDREW.—Midshipman of the *Griper*, (Liddon,) 1819-20. Lieutenant in the *Fury*, (Parry), 1821-23.

> Accompanied Parry in his journey across Melville Island.

REID, JOHN.—An old whaling Captain, native of Aberdeen. Ice-master of the *Erebus*, (Franklin,) 1845-48.

Renwick, C. K.—Engineer of the *Phœnix*, (Inglefield,) 1853.

Reynolds, P.—Carpenter of the *Discovery*, (Clarke,) 1779-80, in Cook's Expedition.

RICARDS, J. R.—Assistant-Surgeon in the *Assistance*, (Belcher,) 1852-54. In the theatricals he acted Mr. Sandford in the " *Irish Tutor.*"

RICHARDS, GEORGE H.—Entered the navy in 1832, and early adopted the surveying branch of the service. He was in the *Sulphur*, (Belcher,) 1836-41. Lieutenant, 1842, in the *Philomel*, (Sulivan,) surveying on the south-east coast of South America. Made Commander in 1845 for services up the Parana. Commander in the *Acheron*, (Stokes,) surveying on the coast of New Zealand. Commander of the *Assistance*, (Belcher,) 1852-54. Manager of the " *Queen's Arctic Theatre*," in 1852-53. The plays acted were " *The Irish Tutor*," and " *Silent Woman*," by the officers, and " *Hamlet* " and the " *Scapegrace* " by the men. In the sledge travelling he was 94 days away, and travelled over 808 miles. After a march of 57 days he reached the *Resolute*, at Melville Island, having taken two boats with him, one left at Cape Franklin, the other on the west shore of Byam Martin Channel. Left the *Resolute* to return on June 8th. From February 22nd to 27th, 1854, he led a sledge party from the *Assistance* to Beechey Island, with the temperature at —40° *Fahr.* Captain, 1854. In the *Plumper* and *Hecate*, employed in the survey of British Columbia and determining the boundary between the dominion of Canada and the United States. On his way home he made considerable additions to the charts of the Mexican coast. Hydrographer 1863-73. Retired Rear-Admiral. C.B., F.R.S., F.R.G.S.

> Appointed in December, 1874, on a Committee (with Admirals Sir L. McClintock and Osborn,) to make preparations for the Arctic Expedition of 1875.

Cape Richards, north point of Sabine Peninsula.

RICHARDS, CHARLES.—Midshipman in the *Fury*, (Parry,) 1821-23. In the company of the " *Royal Arctic Theatre.*" Acted Mrs.

Malaprop in the "*Rivals.*" Accompanied Parry on his journey in 1822, when he discovered Fury and Hecla Strait. In the *Hecla*, (Parry,) 1824-25.

Richards Bay near the south entrance of Fury and Hecla Strait.

RICHARDS, CHARLES.—Clerk in the *Assistance*, (Ommanney,) 1850-51. Acted First Officer in *Charles XII*. Lost in the Nerbudda.

Richards Point in Ommanny Bay, Prince of Wales' Land.

RICHARDS, W. H.—Brother of the above, clerk in charge of the *Resolute*, (Kellett,) 1852-54. Now Paymaster in the *Bellerophen*, (West Indies).

Richards, William T.—Clerk in charge of the *Phœnix*, (Inglefield,) 1853 and 1854. Paymaster 1854, of the *Audacious*, (Colomb,) 1874.

RICHARDSON, JOHN.—Was born at Dumfries in 1787. Entered the navy as an Assistant-Surgeon in 1807. Surgeon, 1809, in the *Hercules*, at the siege of Tarragona, and with Sir George Cockburn in the American war. In 1819 he joined Franklin in his land expedition, and descended the Copper-mine to the sea. In the second Franklin expedition of 1825-28, Richardson explored 903 miles of the Arctic sea between the Mackenzie and the Copper-mine. 1840, Inspector of Haslar Hospital. C.B. *Knighted*, 1846. F.R.S. F.R.G.S. In 1848 he descended the Mackenzie in search of Franklin, and examined the coast thence to the Copper-mine. He assisted in the equipment of the other searching expeditions by preparing pemmican and antiscorbutics. He retired to Grassmere, where he died on June 5th, 1866, aged 77. He was the author of "*Fauna Boreali Americana*," (2 vols. folio, 1829 to 1836,) "*Report on North American Zoology*," (8vo. 1837,) "*On the Frozen soil of North America*," (8vo. 1841,) the article on the Polar Regions in the Encyclopœdia Britannica; "*Arctic Searching Expedition*," (2 vols., 8vo., 1851,) "*The Polar Regions*," (Edinburgh, 1861).

Rickman, John.—Second Lieutenant of the *Discovery*, Clarke, 1776-79, in Cook's expedition.

ROBERTSON, W.—Surgeon in the *Enterprise*, (J. C. Ross,) 1848-49.

ROBERTSON, J.—Surgeon of the *Terror*, (Crozier,) in the Antarctic Expedition, 1839-43.

ROBINSON, F.—Second Lieutenant of the *Investigator*, (Bird,) 1848-49. Went with a travelling party from Port Leopold to Fury Beach.

ROCHE, RICHARD.—Midshipman in the *Herald*, (Kellett,) 1845-51. Mate in the *Resolute*, (Kellett,) 1852-54. In the sledge travelling of 1853 he was 78 days away from the ship, on various occasions as auxiliary, and went over 798 miles. He is now commander of H.M.S. *Hibernia*, at Malta.

Roche Point, on the northwest coast of Sabine Peninsula.

ROSS, JOHN.—Was born in 1777, at Balsaroch, in Wigtonshire, and entered the navy in 1786; serving much under Sir James Saumarez. In three actions he was wounded 13 times. Commander, 1812; of the *Isabella*, 1818, and commanding the expedition. In 1829 he again sailed in the *Victory*, steamer, discovered Boothia, and returned in 1833. F.R.G.S., and *Gold Medallist*, R.G.S., 1834, and of Paris G.S. Created C.B. and Knight of the Pole Star of Sweden. *Knighted*, 1834. Consul at Stockholm, 1838. Rear-Admiral, 1851. In the *Felix*, schooner, in the search for Franklin, 1850-51. He died in November, 1856. [*See Obituary ·Notice in R.G.S.J., vol. xxviii., p. cxxx.*) Sir John Ross was author of " *Voyage of discovery for the purpose of exploring Baffin's Bay*," (1819.) " *Narrative of a Second Voyage in search of a North West Passage, including " The Discovery of the North Magnetic Pole*," (1835). " *The last voyage of Captain Sir John Ross to the Arctic Regions, by R. Huish*," (1835,) was published by one of the crew of the *Victory*.

ROSS, JAMES CLARK.—Born in 1800 and entered the navy in April, 1812, in the *Briseis*, commanded by his uncle, John Ross. Midshipman in the *Isabella*, (J. Ross,) 1818, in the *Hecla*, (Parry,) 1819-20. In the company of the *Royal Arctic Theatre*. Acted Corinna in *The Citizen*, Mrs. Bruin in the *Mayor of Garratt*, Ann Lovely in a *Bold Stroke for a Wife*, and Poll in the *N. W. Passage*. In the *Fury*, (Parry,) 1821-23, Second Lieutenant in the *Fury*, (Hoppner,) 1824-25. Went on a travelling party in July, from Port Bowen along the coast to the north. First Lieutenant of the *Hecla*, (Parry,) 1827; and in the second boat when they reached 82° 45'. N. With his uncle in the *Victory*, 1829-33. *On June 1st, 1831, he planted the Union Jack on the North Magnetic Pole.* Captain, 1834. In 1835 he was employed on the magnetic survey of Great Britain. In 1836, he fitted out the *Cove* at Hull in winter, and went to Davies Strait in search of missing whalers. 1837-38 on the magnetic survey of the coast of Great Britain. Captain of the *Erebus*, 1839-43, in command of the Antarctic Expedition. Captain of the *Enterprise*, 1848-49, in search of Sir John Franklin. In the sledge travelling to explore the north and west shores of North Somerset, he was away 40 days, going over 500 miles, a feat unprecedented at that time. He was knighted in 1844. D.C.L. *Gold Medal*, R.G.S. 1842. F.R.S. F.L.S. He died at Aylesbury on April 3rd, 1861, aged 61. He was author of " *The Position of the Magnetic Pole,*" (1834,) and " *Voyage of discovery and research in the Antarctic Regions,*" (2 vols., 8vo., 1847). [*See Obituary Notice, proceedings R.S., xii., p. lxi.*

Cape James Ross, south entrance of Liddon's Gulf.

Strait of James Ross, between Boothia and King William Island.

James Ross Peninsula, south of Boothia Isthmus.

Ross Island, the most northern of the Spitzbergen group.

ROSS, M. G.—First Lieutenant of the *Investigator,* (Bird,) 1848-49.

ROWLAND, WILLIAM.—Assistant-Surgeon in the *Griper,* (Clavering,) 1823 ; and in the *Hecla,* (Parry,) 1824-25.

Rudall, James T.—Acting Assistant-Surgeon of the *Talbot,* (Jenkins,) 1854. He left the service.

RUTTER, J.—Clerk in charge of the *North Star,* (Saunders,) 1849-50.

RYDER, J. N.—First Engineer of the *Intrepid,* (Cator,) 1850-51. He left the service and worked at Messrs. Penn and Co., at Greenwich. He died in 1864. F.R.G.S.

SABESTER, JOHN.—Ice Master in the *North Star,* (Saunders,) 1849-50.

SABINE, EDWARD.—Born in 1788. Lieutenant, R.A. ; served in Canada during the American war. In the *Isabella,* (J. Ross,) 1818, for magnetic and pendulum observations ; and in the *Hecla,* (Parry,) 1819-20. In the company of the *Royal Arctic Theatre.* Acted Lord Minnikin in *Bon Ton,* and Freeman in a *Bold Stroke for a Wife.* Editor of the " *North Georgia Gazette,*" an Arctic Newspaper. Accompanied Parry on his journey across Melville Island. Conducted a series of pendulum observations in the *Pheasant,* in the Atlantic ; and at Spitzbergen, and on the east coast of Greenland in the *Griper,* (Clavering,) 1827. Captain, 1813. Lieutenant-Colonel, 1841. Colonel, 1851. Major-General, 1859. General Secretary to the British Association for 20 years. President, 1853. F.R.S., 1818. President of the Royal Society, 1861-73. D.C.L., L.L.D. K.C.B., 1869. F.R.G.S. Author of " *Account of Experiments to determine the figure of the Earth by means of the pendulum vibrating seconds in different*

latitudes," with a brief account of Clavering's voyage to Spitz-bergen in 1827 ; and of numerous reports on magnetic observations.
Sabine Peninsula, northern part of Melville Island.

SAINSBURY, H. H.—Mate in the *Investigator*, (McClure,) 1850-54. He died on board the *Resolute*, on November 14th, 1853.

SARGENT, ROBERT O.—Mate of the *Erebus*, (Franklin,) 1845-48.
" A nice pleasant-looking lad, very good natured."—*Fitzjames*.
Point Sargent on the east coast of Bathurst Island.

SAUNDERS, JAMES.—Master of the *Terror*, (Back,) 1836-37 ; and Master commanding the *North Star*, 1849-50.
Saunders Island in the entrance of Wolstenholme Sound.

SCALLON, JAMES.—Gunner in the *Hecla*, (Parry,) 1819-20; in the *Fury*, (Parry,) 1821-23.

SCOTT, ROBERT C.—Assistant Surgeon in the *Resolute*, (Kellett,) 1852-54. Accompanied McClintock across Melville Island, in the autumn travelling of 1852, 38 days away, and went over 225 miles. Now Staff-Surgeon of the *Clyde*, naval reserve at Aberdeen.

Seemann, Berthold—Naturalist of the *Herald*, (Kellett,) 1845-51. Author of " *Narrative of the Voyage of H.M.S. Herald, and Three Cruises in the Arctic Regions in search of Sir J. Franklin,*" (2 vols., 8vo., 1853). F.R.G.S. He died on October 10th, 1871, at the Javali gold mines, in Nicaragua. [*See Obituary Notice R.G.S.J.. vol. xlii., p. clxvii.*]

Seymour, Edward Hobort.—Nephew of Sir Michael Seymour. Made a voyage to the Spitzbergen seas in a whaler in 1868, with Captain Gray. Captain, 1872.

Sheddon, Robert A.—A volunteer searcher for Sir John Franklin's expedition up Behring's Strait, in the yacht, *Nancy Dawson*. He was formerly a Mate in the Navy. Went nearly to Point Barrow in 1849. He died at Mazatlan in October, 1849.

SHELLABEER, W.—Master's Assistant in the *Enterprise*, (J. C. Ross,) 1848-49. Second Master in the *Intrepid*, (Cator,) 1850-51. Acted Second Officer, in *Charles XII*. Led an auxiliary sledge party to supply Lieutenant McClintock. 24 days away, and marched 245 miles. In the *North Star*, (Pullen,) 1852-54.

SKEOCH, J.—Assistant-Surgeon in the *Fury*, (Parry,) 1821-23.
Skeoch Bay, on south coast of Cockburn Island.

SHERER, JOSEPH.—Son of the Rev. J. G. Sherer, Vicar of Westwell, in Kent. Born in 1798. Entered the Navy in 1811. Midshipman in the *Hecla*, (Lyon,) 1821-23. Acted Lydia Languish in the *Rivals*. Lieutenant in the *Hecla*, (Parry,) 1824-25. In the autumn of 1824 he killed a "payable" whale. Went on a travelling party, in July, from Port Bowen along the coast to the south. In 1828 he obtained command of the *Monkey*, schooner, in the West Indies, and captured the Spanish schooner *Josepha*, with 207 slaves; also the Spanish brig *Midas*, with 420 slaves, after an action of 35 minutes. He then received command of the *Nimble*, schooner, and captured the *Gallito*, with 136 slaves. Commander, 1829, and made a Knight of the Guelphic Order by William IV. Commander of the Coastguard, 1831-37. In February, 1838, appointed to the *Dee*, steamer, on the North American Station. Captain, 1841. Now a retired Vice-Admiral.

Mount Sherer, south of Port Bowen.

Sherer Creek in Lyon Inlet (Melville Peninsula).

SIBBALD, J.—Second Lieutenant of the *Erebus*, (J. C. Ross,) in the Antarctic Expedition, 1839-41. First Lieutenant of the *Terror*, (Crozier,) 1842-43. Commander, 1843. Afterwards Secretary to the Governor of the Falkland Islands. Since deceased.

SIMPSON, J.—Surgeon of the *Plover*, (Moore,) 1848-51, and 1852-54. In the boat expedition to Point Barrow. Author of "*Results of Thermometrical Observations made at the Plover's Wintering Place, Point Barrow*," (8vo., 1857); and of a valuable report on the Tuski and Western Eskimo. Invalided and returned to England in 1851, but he rejoined the *Plover*, with Captain Maguire, in 1852. Died at Haslar in 1858.

SKEAD, F.—Second Master in the *Enterprise*, (Collinson.) Afterwards on the Cape of Good Hope Survey. Now a retired Navigating Lieutenant, and Harbour Master at Port Elizabeth, Cape Colony.

Skene, J. M.—Midshipman in the *Isabella*, (Ross,) 1818.

SKENE, A. M.—Midshipman in the *Griper*, (Liddon,) 1819-20.

Skene Bay on the south shore of Melville Island.

SMITH, A. J.—Mate and Lieutenant in the *Erebus*, (J. C. Ross), 1839-43, in the Antarctic Expedition. Afterwards at the Magnetic Observatory at Hobart Town. He died, a retired Commander, at Melbourne, 1873.

E

Smith, Benjamin Leigh.— A volunteer Arctic explorer. In 1871 he sailed with a view to attaining a high latitude, and exploring the unknown parts of Spitzbergen. He went down Hinlopen Strait in August, visited the Seven Islands in September, and discovered that North East Land had a much greater eastern prolongation than was previously supposed. He afterwards attained a latitude of 81° 24′ N. In 1872 he made a second voyage to Spitzbergen in his yacht *Samson*, and in 1873 another in the steamer *Diana*. F.R.G.S. Knight of the Pole Star of Sweden.

SMITH, JOHN.—Carpenter of the *Terror*, (Back,) 1824-25.

SMITH, WILLIAM.—Boatswain of the *Hecla*, (Parry,) 1824-25.

Smith, John.—A mate in the *Cove*, (J. C. Ross,) 1836.

SMITH, JOHN.—Clerk in charge of the *Prince Albert*, (Kennedy,) 1851-52.

SMYTH, WILLIAM H.—Entered the navy in 1813. Mate in the *Blossom*, (Beechey,) 1825-28. Lieutenant in the *Samarang*, (Paget,) in the Pacific, crossed the Andes, and made a voyage down the Amazon, 1831-35. First Lieutenant of the *Terror*, (Back,) 1836-37. Manager of the "*Royal Arctic Theatre*," 1836-37, composed the prologue and several songs. The plays acted were "*Monsieur Tonson*" by the officers, and the "*First Floor*" and the "*Benevolent Tar*," by the men. He also superintended the evening school. The beautiful illustrations in Back's Narrative are from his sketches. Commander of the *Grecian*, in South America, 1838-43. He has not served since. F.R.G.S. He is author of "*Narrative of a Journey from Lima to Para*," (1836). Now a retired Vice-Admiral. He is an admirable artist.

　　Smyth Harbour, near the entrance of Frozen Strait, in Southampton Island.

Speer, Denton.—Second Master of the *Talbot*, (Jenkins,) 1854. Since deceased.

Snow, W. Parker.—In the *Prince Albert*, (Forsyth,) 1850. Author of "*Voyage of the Prince Albert in search of Sir J. Franklin*," (1851).

　　Parker Snow Point, to the south of Cape Dudley Digges (Greenland).

STANLEY, OWEN.—Son of the Bishop of Norwich, born in 1811, and entered the navy in 1824. He adopted the surveying branch of the service, and served in the *Adventure*, (King,) in

Magellan's Straits, and under Captain Graves in the Mediter-
ranean. Second Lieutenant of the *Terror*, (Back,) 1836-37.
Drew the map for the Narrative of Back's Voyage, 1836-37.
Captain, 1844, of the *Rattlesnake*, in Australia, surveying
Torres Strait, and the Louisiade Archipelago. F.R.G.S. He
died at Sydney on March 13th, 1850. [*See Obituary Notice*,
R.G.S.J., vol. xxvi., p. lix.]

> *Stanley Harbour* off Southampton Island.

STANLEY, S.—In the *Cornwallis* during the China War, 1840. Surgeon
of the *Erebus*, (Franklin,) 1845-48.

STEVENSON, W. C.—Master's Assistant of the *Plover*, (Moore,) 1848-
50, in the boat expedition from Point Barrow, and rejoined
in 1853. In the *Rattlesnake*, (Trollope,) 1854.

STEWART, J.—Commander of the *Sophia*, brig, belonging to Penny's
expedition, 1850-51. Afterwards commanded a large steam
transport in the Black Sea, during the Crimean war.

> *Stewart Bay* on the north coast of Cornwallis Island.

SUTHERLAND, PETER C.—Surgeon of the *Sophia*, (Stewart,) 1850-51.
Author of "*Journal of a Voyage in Baffin's Bay and Barrows
Straits, with a Narrative of Sledge Excursions,*" (2 vols, 8vo.,
1852). Afterwards, for many years, Surveyor-General at Port
Natal.

> *Sutherland Island* on the east coast of Wellington Channel.

SUTHERLAND, KENNETH.—Carpenter of the *Prince Albert*, (Kennedy,)
1851-52.

SWANSEA, JACOB.—Boatswain in the *Hecla*, (Parry,) 1819-20.

TATHAM, W.—Master of the *Investigator*, (Bird,) 1848-49.

TAYLOR, G.—Third Mate of the *Victory*, (Ross,) 1829-33.

TAYLOR, J.—Boatswain of the *Assistance*, (Belcher,) 1852-54.

TERRY, THOMAS.—A Warrant Officer of the *Erebus*, (Franklin,)
1845-48.

THOM, W.—Purser of the *Isabella*, (Ross,) 1818 ; and of the *Victory*,
(Ross,) 1829-33. On his return made Purser of the *Canopus*.

> *Thom's Bay*, in Boothia Felix.

THOMAS, ROBERT.—Mate in the *Terror*, (Crozier,) 1845-48.

THOMAS, CHIMHAM.—Carpenter of H.M.S. *Eurydice*. Volunteered
as Carpenter of the *Victory*, (Ross,) 1829-33. He died and

was buried at Fury Beach, in February, 1833. (See *Mark-ham's Whaling Cruise in Baffin's Bay, p. 231*).

THOMPSON, JAMES.—A Warrant Officer of the *Terror*, (Crozier,) 1845-48.

Tom, John.—Midshipman in the *Griper*, (Lyon,) 1824. Lieutenant, 1826 to 1846.

TOMS, F. Y.—Assistant-Surgeon in the *Assistance*, (Belcher,) and the *North Star*, (Pullen,) 1852-54. Surgeon, 1857. Now Staff-Surgeon of the *Invincible*, in the Mediterranean.
> *Toms Point*, at N.W. end of Bathurst Island.

TRACEY, J.—Master's-Assistant in the *Investigator*, (Bird,) 1848-49. Now a merchant in Bombay.

TUCKER, CHARLES T.—Master of the *Erebus*, (J. C. Ross,) 1839-43, in the Antarctic Expedition. Now a retired Staff-Commander. Serving under the Thames Conservancy.

TROLLOPE, H.—Lieutenant of the *Herald*, 1845-51). Commander of the *Rattlesnake*, 1853. Wintered in Port Clarence, Behring Strait, 1853-54. Now a retired Captain.

TUFNELL, N. G.—Midshipman in the *Pagoda*, in the Antarctic Expedition of 1845.

VERNON, CHARLES E. H.—Born in 1827. Lieutenant in the *Plover*, (Maguire,) 1852. Afterwards Commander of the *Cordelia*, in Australia and the East Indies. He died in 1873.

Wainwright, J.—Clerk of the *Blossom*, (Beechey,) 1825-28.
> *Wainwright Inlet*, north of Icy Cape.

WALLIS, WM.—Carpenter in the *Hecla*, (Parry,) 1819-20.

WAKEHAM, CYRUS.—Clerk of the *Dorothea*, (Buchan,) 1818, and of the *Griper*, (Liddon,) 1819-20. Composed several Arctic songs ; the Opening Address and the Farewell Address for the Theatre. Acted Puff in "*Miss in her Teens*" ; Beaufort in "*The Citizen*" ; Bruin in "*The Mayor of Garratt*" ; Obediah Prim in "*A bold stroke for a Wife*" ; and Dick in the "*N. W. Passage.*"

Walden, John.—Midshipman of the *Racehorse*, (Phipps,) 1773.
> *Walden Island*, off the north coast of Spitzbergen.

WALKER, DAVID.—A native of Belfast. Surgeon of the *Fox*, (McClintock,) 1857-59. Author of papers "*On the forma-*

tion of Sea Ice," and *" On the Zoology of the Fox Expedition, in the Proceedings of the Royal Society of Dublin.* Now in the United States Army.

WARD, JOHN.—Assistant-Surgeon of the *Intrepid,* (Cãtor,) 1850-51.

WEBB, H. P.—Second-Engineer of the *Pioneer,* (Osborn,) 1850-51. In the sledge travelling, volunteered and worked as one of the men in Osborn's sledge.

> *Webb Point,* on the west coast of Prince of Wales' Land.

Webber, Mr.—Artist, *Resolution,* (Cook).

WEDDELL, JAMES.—Master R.N. Made a voyage to the Antarctic Ocean in 1822-24, and reached 74° S.

> Author of *" A Voyage towards the South Pole"* (8vo, 1827).

WEEKES, JOHN.—A Warrant Officer of the *Erebus,* (Franklin,) 1845-48.

WELLER, C. C.—Midshipman of the *Fury,* (Hoppner,) 1824-25.

Wells, John C.—Retired Commander. Went for a cruise to Spitzbergen with Mr. Leigh Smith, 1872.

> Author of *" The Gateway to the Polynia.—A Voyage to Spitzbergen"* (1873).

WENTWORTH, W.—Boatswain of the *Fury,* (Hoppner,) 1824-25.

WESTROPP, B.—Midshipman in the *Fury,* (Hoppner,) 1824-25. Lieutenant, 1825. Left the service for an appointment as Secretary of the Humane Society.

Whiffin, J. G.—Clerk in the *Herald,* (Kellett,) 1845-51. Since constantly employed until his retirement.

Wilcox, J.—Second Greenland Pilot in the *Isabella,* (Ross,) 1818.

> *Wilcox Head,* south of the Devil's Thumb, Melville Bay (Greenland).

Williamson, John.—Third Lieutenant of the *Resolution,* (Cook,) 1776-1779.

Wolfe, J.—Mate in the *Blossom,* (Beechey,) 1825-28. Afterwards employed for many years on the Home Surveys.

WOOD, J. F. L.—Lieutenant in the *Erebus,* (J. C. Ross,) 1839-41, and *Terror,* (Crozier,) 1842-43, in the Antarctic Expedition. Commander, 1843. Afterwards Secretary to the Mendicity Society.

Woodward, J.—Purser in the *Herald,* (Kellett,) 1845-51. He died on the passage home in January, 1851.

Wright, Arthur R.—Lieutenant in the *Talbot*, (Jenkins,) 1854. Commander, 1864.

WRIGHT, T. D.—Midshipman in the *Plover*, (Maguire,) 1852-53. Passed one winter at Point Barrow and then invalided.

WYNN, J. LAND—First Lieutenant of the *Hecla*, (Parry,) 1824-25.

WYNNIATT, ROBERT.—Midshipman in the *Samarang*, (Belcher,) 1843-47. Mate in the *Investigator*,(M'Clure,)1850-54. In sledge travelling he was absent from May 6th to June 7th, 1851. He went to the furthest east point of the north shore of Prince Albert Land (26th May, 1851,) separated by a strait from Osborn's furthest west point on Prince of Wales Land', 40 miles apart. Went home in the *Phœnix*, 1853.

YOUNG, ALLEN.—Entered the merchant service in 1846. Commanded the *Marlborough*, East Indiaman, (1500 tons,) twice round the world, 1853-54; and the *Adelaide*, steam troop ship 3,000 tons, during the Crimean war, 1855-56. Sailing-Master of the *Fox*, (McClintock,) 1857-59. Commenced his travelling work by laying out a depôt between February 15th and March 3rd, blowing a gale of wind and the thermometer averaging —40 to —48. Mercury frozen all the time. On his return he started for Fury Beach to get some stores left by Parry, absent from March 18th to 28th. Attacked with snow blindness. Started again on April 7th, tracing the south and west shores of Prince of Wales' Land. After 38 days he sent back the men and tent, owing to provisions running short. Went on for 40 days, with one man and the dogs, sleeping each night in a hole in the snow. He attempted to cross the McClintock Channel, and went about 40 miles from the land, the ice being frightfully heavy. Reached the ship on June 7th, after an absence of 78 days. Went again to explore Peel Sound from June 10th to 28th. He then connected Osborn's with Browne's furthest, and discovered 380 miles of new coast line. Became a Lieutenant of the Naval Reserve, February 24th, 1862. F.R.G.S. Commanded the *Fox*, in the North Atlantic Telegraph Expedition in 1862, going to Farœ Isles, Iceland, and Greenland. Commanded the *Quantung*, gunboat, belonging to the European Chinese Navy, 1862-64. Commissioner to the Maritime Congress at Naples, in 1871.

Author of an account of the voyage of the *Fox*, in the first number of the Cornhill Magazine.

Allen Young Point, the south-west extreme of Prince of Wales' Land.

Young, Walter.—Lieutenant commanding the brig *Lion*, sent to meet Captain Cook by way of Baffin's Bay, in 1777. Reached the Woman's Islands, and returned in August. He died in the West Indies in 1781, when Captain of H.M.S. *Sandwich*, Rodney's flag-ship.

YULE, HENRY B.—Second Master in the *Erebus*, (J. C. Ross,) 1829-33, in the Antarctic Expedition. Afterwards employed in the Home Survey. Now a retired Staff-Commander.

ADDENDA.

AYLEN, JOHN F. R.—Master's Assistant in the *North Star*, (Saunders,) 1849-50. Made the survey of North Star Bay in Wolstenholme Sound. Now Staff-Commander of the *Asia*, steam-reserve at Portsmouth.

OSBORNE, MR.—Boatswain of the *Investigator*, (Bird,) 1848-49, and of the *Assistance*, (Ommanney,) 1850-51. Formerly Captain of the Maintop of the *Fisgard*, (Duntze,) in the Pacific, 1842-46.

SHIPS · REFERRED TO

IN THE FOREGOING LIST. *

Alexander.—1818, (Parry). Ross's first expedition. A summer cruise in Baffin's Bay. 252 tons.

*ASSISTANCE.—1850-51, (Ommanney). Franklin search. Wintered off Griffith Island. 430 tons. 60 officers and men. No deaths. (Austin's Expedition).

1852-54, (Belcher). Franklin search. First winter in Northumberland Sound ; second, Wellington Channel. Two deaths. *Abandoned* 1854.

Blossom.—1825-28, (Beechey). Two summer cruises in Behring Strait.

---

* Vessels in *italics*, only made summer cruises ; those in SMALL CAPITALS, wintered ; those with * were abandoned.

*Breadalbane.—1853, (Fawckner). Transport, run over by the ice, off Beechey Island.

Carcass.—1773, (Lutwidge). Summer cruise to Spitzbergen.

Cove.—1836, (J. C. Ross). Hired at Hull, to relieve whalers in Davis Straits.

Discovery.—1776-80, (Clerke and Gore). Second ship in Cook's Third Expedition. Summer cruises in Behring Strait. 300 tons. 80 officers and men.

Dorothea.—1818, (Buchan). Summer cruise to Spitzbergen.

ENTERPRISE.—1848-49, (J. C. Ross). Franklin search. Wintered at Port Leopold. 530 tons. 63 officers and men. Lost one officer (Mr. Mathias, the Assistant-Surgeon,) and three men.

    1850-54, (Collinson). Franklin search, by Behring Strait. First winter in a Sound on Prince Albert's Land, in 71° 35′ N. 1851-52; second at Cambridge Bay, 1852-53 ; third at Camden Bay, 1853-54. She returned May 6th, 1855. Lost three men, one in each year.

*EREBUS.—1839-43, (J. C. Ross,) in the Antarctic Expedition. 370 tons. 64 officers and men.

    1845-48, (Franklin). To discover the N.W. Passage. 65 officers and men. First winter at Beechey Island, 1845-46. Lost two men. Second and third winters in the pack, north of King William Island in 70° 5′ N. 1846-47-48. Lost nine officers and twelve men (including the *Terror's* losses), from 1846 to April 1848. Ship *abandoned* April 22nd, 1848, when 105 souls landed on King William Island.

FOX.—1857-59, (McClintock). Franklin Search. First winter in the Baffin's Bay Pack. Lost one man in consequence of a fall. Second winter in Brentford Bay. Lost two men. Screw yacht of 177 tons. 26 officers and men.

FELIX.—1850-51, (J. Ross). Franklin Search. Small schooner. Wintered in Assistance Bay, Cornwallis Island. No deaths.

*FURY.—1821-23, (Parry). 377 tons. 60 officers and men. First winter at Winter Island. Lost one man from a fall from aloft. Second winter at Igloolik. Lost two petty officers (Greenland Mates).

    1824-25, (Hoppner). 60 officers and men. Wintered at Port Bowen. No deaths. August, 1825, ship driven on shore by the ice and *abandoned.*

GRIPER.—1819-20, (Liddon). Gun brig of 180 tons. 36 officers and men. Wintered at Melville Island. No deaths.

1823, (Clavering). Summer cruise to Spitzbergen and Greenland. No deaths.

1824, (Lyon). Summer cruise towards Repulse Bay, by Roe's Welcome. No deaths.

HECLA.—1819-20, (Parry). 375 tons. 58 officers and men. Wintered at Melville Island. One man died.

1821-23, (Lyon). 62 officers and men. First winter at Winter Island. Lost two men in June, 1822. Second winter at Igloolik, No deaths.

1824-25, (Parry.) Winter at Port Bowen. No deaths.

1827, (Parry). Summer cruise to Spitzbergen, in the attempt to reach the Pole. No deaths.

Herald.—1845-51, (Kellett). 500 tons. 110 officers and men. Three summer cruises up Behring Strait. One death.

*INTREPID.—1850-51, (Cator). Franklin search. Screw steamer, 430 tons, 60 H.P. 24 officers and men. Wintered off Griffith Island. No deaths. (Austin's Expedition.)

1852-54, (McClintock). Franklin search. First winter at Dealy Island (Melville Island). Lost two men. Second winter in the pack. Lost two men. *Abandoned* 1854. (Kellett's Expedition).

*INVESTIGATOR.—1848-49, (Bird). Franklin search. 538 tons, 60 officers and men. Wintered at Port Leopold. Lost two men.

1850-53, (M'Clure). Franklin search. First winter at Princess Royal Islands. No deaths. Second and third at Bay of Mercy. No deaths until April, 1853, when three men died. Mr. Sainsbury (Mate), died on board the *Resolute*, in November, 1853, and one man on board the *North Star*, 1854. Ship *abandoned*, 1853.

Isabel.—1852, (Inglefield). Screw schooner. 149 tons. A summer cruise in Baffin's Bay. No deaths.

LADY FRANKLIN.—1850-51, (Penny). Franklin search. A brig. Wintered in Assistance Bay, Cornwallis Island. No deaths.

Lion.—1776-77, (Pickersgill and Young). Brig sent to meet Captain Cook up Baffin's Bay. Never went beyond the Woman Islands.

NORTH STAR.—1849-50, (Saunders).   Store ship.   Franklin search. Wintered at Wolstenholme Sound.   Lost four men.

　　1852-54 (Pullen).   Store ship.   Franklin search.   Wintered at Beechey Island.   No deaths.

PAGODA.—A barque hired at the Cape to complete some magnetic and other work after the return of Sir James Ross's Antarctic Expedition.   She was officered and manned from H.M.S. *Winchester*, flag ship at the Cape.   She left Simon's Bay in January, 1845, and returned in June, having reached 69° S. where she was stopped by impenetrable pack ice.

Phœnix.—1853, (Inglefield).   Steam   transport.   Summer trip to Beechey Island.   No deaths.

　　1854, (Inglefield).   Summer trip to Beechey Island. Brought home part of the Belcher Expedition.

*PIONEER.—1850-51, (Osborn).   Screw steamer, 430 tons, 60 horse-power.   24 officers and men.   Franklin search.   Wintered off Griffith Island.   No deaths.   (Austin's Expedition).

　　1852-54, (Osborn).   Franklin   search.   Wintered at Northumberland Sound.   No deaths.   Second winter in Wellington Channel.   No deaths.   Ship *abandoned*, 1854.

PLOVER.—1848-50, (Moore).   Store ship.   Complement 41 men, 213 tons.   Franklin search.   Wintered at Kotzebue Sound, 1849-50, and at Port Clarence, 1850-51, and 1851-52.   A fresh commission 1852-54, (Maguire).   Wintered at Point Barrow 1852-53, and 1853-54.   In 1854 the *Plover* was condemned and sold at San Francisco.*

PRINCE ALBERT.—1850, (Forsyth).   Schooner.   89 tons.   Summer cruise to Prince Regent's Inlet.   Franklin search.   No deaths.

　　1851-52, (Kennedy).   Franklin search.   Wintered in Batty Bay.   No deaths.

Racehorse.—1773, (Phipps).   92 officers and men.   Summer cruise to Spitzbergen.

*RESOLUTE.—1850-51, (Austin).   410 tons.   60 officers and men. Franklin search.   Wintered off Griffith Island.   One death in the spring, from frost bite.

---

　　*A vessel from the Pacific squadron communicated with the *Plover* each year, after the departure of the *Herald*.   In 1851 H.M.S *Dædalus*, (Captain Wellesley,) was sent to Port Clarence on this duty.   The *Amphitrite* (Captain Frederick,) took up Captain Maguire in 1852, and went as far as Icy Cape again in 1853.   H.M.S. *Rattlesnake* (Captain Trollope,) also brought up supplies in 1853 ; and the *Trincomalee*, (Captain Houston,) in 1854.

1852-54, (Kellett). Franklin search. First winter at Dealy Island (Melville Isle). One death. Second winter in the Pack, in 74° 41′ N. One death. In 1852-53-54, the aggregate distance walked over by 13 officers of the *Resolute*, and *Intrepid* was 13,337 geographical miles ; and the quantity of new coast line discovered was 1,618 miles. They obtained, by shooting, 28,254 lbs. of fresh meat. The force employed was 88 officers and men, and 10 dogs. *Abandoned* May 13th, 1854. On September 10th, 1855, she was picked up (having drifted out of Baffin's Bay, upwards of 1,100 miles) in 67° N. Lat., by the American Whaler *George Henry* (Captain Buddington). Now laid up in the Medway.

Resolution.—1776-80, (Cook and Clerke). 462 tons. 112 officers and men. Discovery ship up Behring Strait.

SOPHIA.—1850-51,(Stewart). Brig. Franklin search. Wintered in Assistance Bay, Cornwallis Island. No deaths.

Talbot.— 1854, (Jenkins). Transport. Summer trip to Beechey Island. Brought home part of the Belcher Expedition. No deaths.

*TERROR.—1836-37, (Back). 340 tons. 60 officers and men. Wintered in the Pack. Three deaths.

1839-43, (Crozier). Antarctic Expedition. 64 officers and men.

1845-48, (Crozier). Second ship of Franklin's Expedition. Lost one man in 1845-46. (See *Erebus*).

Trent.—1818, (Franklin). Summer cruise to Spitzbergen.

*VICTORY.—1829-33, (J. Ross). Paddle-wheel steamer. 85 tons. 23 officers and men. Three winters on the coast of Boothia. First winter, one death. Second and third winters, no deaths. *Abandoned* 1832. 1832-33, crew wintered at Furv Beach. One death, the carpenter, in February, 1833.

Arctic Expedition of 1875.

OFFICERS.

*(Those with * will be in the advance ship).*

*NARES, GEORGE S., F.R.G.S.—Captain, 10th December, 1869. Commanding the Expedition. *See page 37.*

STEPHENSON, HENRY F.—Captain, January 6th, 1875. Commanded H.M. Gun-boat *Heron*, on the Lakes of Canada during Fenian disturbances, from March 5th, 1866, until January, 1867. Flag-Lieutenant to Sir H. Keppel in China. Promoted to a death vacancy, 1868. Commander of the *Rattler* when lost on the coast of Japan, 1869. Commander of the Royal Yacht, 1871-74.

*MARKHAM, ALBERT H., F.R.G.S.—Commander, 29th November, 1872. *See page 34.*

*ALDRICH, PELHAM.—Lieutenant, 11th September, 1866. In the *Scout*, in the Pacific. Flag-Lieutenant to Admiral Key, at Malta. First Lieutenant of the *Challenger*, (Nares,) 1872-74. Nephew of Captain R. Aldrich. *See page 1.*

BEAUMONT, LEWIS A.—Entered the service in 1862. Sub-Lieutenant in the Royal Yacht. Lieutenant, 23rd August, 1867. In the *Blanche*, (Montgomerie,) on the Australian Station, 1868-71. He then qualified for Gunnery Lieutenant, and was appointed as Instructor in the Torpedo Experiments. September 4th, 1874, selected as Gunnery Lieutenant of the *Lord Warden*, flag-ship in the Mediterranean.

*PARR, ALFRED A. C.—Entered the navy 1864, in the *Victoria*, (Goodenough,) flag-ship of Sir Robert Smart in the Mediterranean, 1864-67. In the *Pylades*, in South America, 1867-70. Lieutenant, 15th June, 1870. *Beaufort Testimonial*, and Commission for best examination of his year. Lieutenant in the *Hercules*, (Sherard Osborn). Gunnery Lieutenant of the *Monarch*, (Hood,) 10th June, 1874.

*GIFFARD, GEORGE A.—Entered the service in 1862, in the *Aurora*, (Sir L. McClintock,) 1863 to 1867 in the West Indies ; in the *Hercules*, (Lord Gilford,) in the Channel squadron, 1868-70. Then in the Royal Yacht. Lieutenant, 18th August, 1870. In the *Niobe*, (Sir L. Loraine,) in the West Indies, 1871-74.

*MAY, WILLIAM H.—Entered the navy, 1864, in the *Victoria*, (Goodenough,) flag-ship of Sir Robert Smart in the Mediterranean,

1864-67. In the *Liffey*, in the West Indies. Sub-Lieutenant in the *Hercules*, and Lieutenant 7th September, 1871. Was studying at the College for Gunnery Lieutenant, and had a good prospect of obtaining a Fellowship, which he relinquished from zeal for Arctic service.

ARCHER, ROBERT H.—Midshipman in the *Galatea*, (H.R.H. the Duke of Edinburgh,) 1857-61. Lieutenant, 20th June, 1872, commission for the best examination of the year. Lieutenant in the *Agincourt*, (flag of Admiral Hornby,) in the Channel squadron, 1872-74.

RAWSON, WYATT.—Entered the navy in 1866, in the *Minotaur*, (Goodenough). Afterwards in the *Narcissus*, (Codrington,) in the flying squadron. During the Ashanti war he was in the *Active*, (Commodore Hewett,) and distinguished himself in the march to Kumasi, with the naval brigade, when he was wounded. Lieutenant, 31st March, 1874.

FULFORD, REGINALD B.—Entered the service in 1864; in H.M.S. *Bristol*, on the west-coast of Africa, 1865-66. In H.M.S. *Royal Alfred*, on the North America and West Indian Stations, 1867-69. In H.M.S. *Monarch*, 1869-70, *Immortalité*, 1870-72, and in the *Cruiser* in the Mediterranean, 1872-74. Lieutenant, 8th August, 1874. He is of the old Devonshire family of Fulford, of Fulford, one of the daughters of which, Mistress Faith Fulford, married John Davis, of Sandrudge, the famous Arctic Navigator and Discoverer of Davis Straits.

*EGERTON, GEORGE LE CLERC.—Entered the service in 1866. Served in the *Liffey*, (Johnson,) in the flying squadron, in the *Ariadne*, (Carpenter,) training-ship, in the *Invincible*, (Soady,) and in the *Bellerophon*, flag-ship, in the West Indies, 1874. Sub-Lieutenant, 15th October, 1872.

CONYBEARE, CRAWFORD, J. M.—Served in the *Liverpool*, (flag-ship of Admiral Hornby,) in the first flying squadron. Sub-Lieutenant, 29th October, 1873.

*COLAN, THOMAS, M.D.—Served as Assistant-Surgeon during the Russian war in the Baltic, including service with the advanced squadron in the ice, in 1856. In 1860 in the China War, at the capture of the Taku Forts, and in the Peiho river. 1873 in the *Rattlesnake*, (Commerell,) during the Ashanti War, for which service he was promoted to Staff-Surgeon, 31st March, 1874. He gained the Gilbert Blane Gold Medal for his Medical Journal kept on the west coast of Africa. 1874, in the *Unicorn*, (Brome,) drill ship at Dundee. Author of a *" Memoir on Parasitic Vegetable Fungi and the Diseases induced by them,"* also of an article on the West Coast of Africa.

NINNIS, BELGRAVE, M.D.—Surgeon, 1st August, 1861, Royal Hospital, Plymouth, 1874.

*Moss, EDWARD L., M.D.—Surgeon, 29th February, 1864. For two years in charge of the Esquimalt Hospital at Vancouver's Island, 1872-74.

COPPINGER, RICHARD W., M.D.—Surgeon, 12th November, 1870. In H.M.S. *Cambridge* since August, 1874.

MITCHELL, THOMAS.—Assistant-Paymaster, 25th June, 1864.

*WHIDDON, EDGAR DE H.—Assistant-Paymaster, 13th March, 1867.

*WOOTTON, JAMES.—Engineer, 27th June, 1867. He was studying at the College.

MELROSE, JAMES.—Engineer, 30th January, 1868.

*PITT, JOHN.—Engineer, 13th February, 1874.

WHITE, GEORGE.—Engineer, 4th April, 1874.

SHIPS

OF THE

ARCTIC EXPEDITION OF 1875.

ALERT.—A steam sloop of 1045, (751) tons, and 381 (100) H.P. She has been strengthened and fitted with new engines and boilers, but retains her old name for Arctic service.

DISCOVERY.—Formerly a steam whaler, the *Bloodhound,* built by Messrs. Stephen and Son, of Dundee. She has received her present name for Arctic service.

GRIFFIN & CO., NAUTICAL PUBLISHERS, 2, THE HARD, PORTSMOUTH, AND 15, COCKSPUR STREET, PALL MALL, LONDON, S.W.

Printed in the United States
By Bookmasters